W9-ARX-405

Joy Ride! 2

Faith-Filled Fun &
Games for Drivetime

Joy Ride! 2

Faith-Filled Fun &
Games for Drivetime

by
Jacqueline Lederman

Tyndale House Publishers, Wheaton, Illinois

Heritage Builders™

JOY RIDE! VOLUME 2

Copyright © 2001 by Focus on the Family. All rights reserved.
International copyright secured.

Library of Congress Cataloging-in-Publication Data

Lederman, Jacqueline.
  Joy ride! : faith-filled fun & games for drivetime / by Jacqueline
Lederman.
      p. cm. —(Heritage builders)
    "A Focus on the Family book"—T.p. verso.
    Includes bibliographical references and indexes.
    ISBN: 1-56179-800-2/volume 2
    1. Games in Christian education. 2. Bible games and puzzles. 3.
Games for travelers. 4. Family recreation. I. Title. II. Series.

  BV1536.3 L43 2000
  249—dc21

                                                00–020638

A Focus on the Family book published by
Tyndale House Publishers, Wheaton, Illinois.

All Scripture quotations, unless otherwise indicated, are taken from the
HOLY BIBLE, NEW INTERNATIONAL VERSION®. Copyright © 1973, 1978,
1984 by the International Bible Society. Used by permission of Zondervan
Publishing House. All rights reserved.

No part of this publication may be reproduced, stored in a retrieval system,
or transmitted in any form or by means—electronic, mechanical, photocopy,
recording, or otherwise—without prior permission of the publisher.

Cover Design: Steve Diggs & Friends, Nashville

Illustrator: Mike Moyers

For Lightwave
Concept Design and Direction: Rick Osborne
Managing Editor: Elaine Osborne
Text Director: K. Christie Bowler
Art Director: Terry Van Roon
Editorial Assistant: Mikal Clarke

Printed in the United States of America

01 02 03 04 05/10 9 8 7 6 5 4 3 2 1

Table of Contents

* Indicates activities that require supplies not normally found in a car.

* Indicates activities that require supplies not normally found in a car.

BUMPER STICKER FUN

BIBLE BAFFLERS

* Indicates activities that require supplies not normally found in a car.

Introduction

Ever heard of a living room on wheels? Well, take a good look at your vehicle.

With:

- this book as a tool,
- a desire to pass godly values to your children, and
- a little determination,

you are all set to turn your driving time into fun learning experiences. Just as you might think of having family nights at home in your living room, you can create those fun learning times in your car.

Joy Ride! Volume Two is designed to help you instill specific Christian and moral values in your children; values that you want your children to grab hold of and learn to live out. Think of a parent and child running a baton relay. The child reaches forward and joyfully grasps the baton that the parent holds out to him or her. This book will help you use your driving time as opportunities to pass on the baton of your personal faith and values to your children. Its activities are organized into three sections: **Fun Times**, **Get 'Em Talking**, and **Bible Bafflers**. Each activity comes with an indication of what length drive and what age range it is best suited for. Each also has a difficulty rating: easy (sometimes indicated by "E"), moderate (sometimes indicated by "M"), or hard (sometimes indicated by "H").

Fun Times includes a variety of games and interactive learning activities, with sections of *General*, *Music/Media Fun*, *Mission: Role-play*, and *Let's Pretend* situations. Some of these activities can be contests if you choose, where you can determine a winner and provide candy treats for prizes. Other activities are simply done for fun, with no real competition involved.

Get 'Em Talking is a section that includes different types of activities aimed at stimulating discussions about a variety of value-oriented topics:

• The *Sticky Situations* section gives your child interesting situations to react to with some crazy and some realistic choices to consider. Follow-up questions are provided to help you talk about why a particular decision was chosen, or what some other related issues might be. Some of the questions are age graded, due to more mature subject matter, so you will want to pay attention to those notations.

• The *Glove Compartment Lessons* section uses objects often found in the car or easily put there ahead of time. You will want to plan for these beforehand to make sure you are prepared for where the lesson is headed and to make sure you have that object in your glove compartment that day.

• *From Here to There* offers parents some possible questions to spur discussions about values when you are heading to a specific place. Check here to get some ideas for things to talk about related to that destination.

• *Bumper Sticker Fun* offers popular slogans to talk about in ways that are related to a faith value. These are followed by open-ended questions to start discussions. Try to become more aware of bumper stickers and other slogans you see that can help you talk about values as well.

Bible Bafflers includes a variety of quizzes, word puzzlers, trivia, fill in the blanks, and so on, that will challenge and increase your Bible knowledge. These require someone to be able to read questions and answers while you are driving. If another parent or adult is not along to do that, an older child will need to read to the rest of the family.

Please note we have put an asterisk (*) beside the titles of activities that require supplies not normally found in a car.

How to Use This Book

First of all, use this book to just have fun! You or your children can leaf through and find something fun to play, talk about, or do. It doesn't have to be a big deal, although you can use this "leafing through" time to build excitement and anticipation. Note that it is best not to turn every car ride into a learning time or the kids will tire of it.

Alternatively, you can choose to be more thoughtful in how you use the book by choosing games, activities, or **Get 'Em Talking** discussions that fit with a particular value you want to address. Look up the value that interests you in the Index to find activities that focus on it. After most activities, you will find thoughts on how you can turn the activity into a discussion of values.

Let your children choose activities some of the time. Other times you will want to plan ahead and lead the activity, such as with the *Glove Compartment Lessons*.

If your children are at different ages or skill levels, we suggest you don't always play the games with the whole family. Doing so would discourage the younger or less skilled ones since the older ones would get all the answers. Give the younger ones their own questions at their skill level. If you are trying to include everyone in the discussion, ask specific children to answer certain questions. Get older children involved as facilitators or coaches to the younger ones, or make them play with a handicap (for example, they have to spell their answers, act them out, or talk backwards).

Remember. Enjoyable learning will stick with your children and they'll ask for more.

Have fun passing on your faith!

Fun
Times

GENERAL

Tongue Twisters

Easy. Any length trip. All ages. Players need a good memory or the ability to read.

Have fun saying these tongue twisters as quickly as you can, as many times in a row as you can. Then pick the correct answer to the question that follows each tongue twister. Use the other questions to get discussions going. If your children are younger (3–6 years), use the shorter version of the tongue twisters (in brackets).

Sometimes you will be able to go faster and repeat the twister more often if you start out saying it slowly to get it in your head. Try making up some of your own tongue twisters, too.

1. Jubilant Joshua and jostling Judahites jumped for joy as God jolted Jericho's gigantic gates. [Joshua jumped for joy as Jericho's gigantic gates jolted.]
   - Did Joshua obey, argue with, or abandon God?
   - What character quality do you think Joshua needed on the seventh day of circling Jericho? Why?
   - What might have happened if Joshua had chosen to do things his way instead of God's? (Joshua 5:18–6:20).
2. Lovely large lions lounged lazily, longing for lunch, as Daniel leisurely loitered, little liking the lightless lair. [Lovely lions longed for lunch as Daniel loitered.]
   - Daniel lived because he prayed and trusted, pranced and twirled, or pitied and tricked?
   - Daniel's daily prayer got him in trouble. What saved him? (Daniel 6).
   - Has doing things God's way ever gotten you in trouble? What happened?
3. John the Baptist behaved bravely, boldly baptizing believers, not in a babbling brook, but in the bustling Jordan. [John the Baptist bravely baptized believers.]

- John's boldness eventually cost him his lips, life, or liver?
- John had the chance to let people treat him like the Messiah and honor him. Why do you think he did not let them do this?
- John always spoke the truth and look where it landed him (Matthew 14:1–12). Was it worth it?
- When would you be tempted to waver on the truth? Why?

4. Peter turned pale and panicked as the prancing rooster piercingly proved Jesus' prediction. [Peter panicked as the rooster proved Jesus' prediction.]
   - When the rooster crowed, Peter remembered Jesus' wallet, Jesus' wardrobe, or Jesus' words?
   - Peter was afraid and tried to protect himself. Did it work? Why or why not? (John 18:15–27).
   - How did Jesus treat Peter after his failure? (John 21:15–23).
   - How do you think Jesus will treat you when you blow it?

5. Muttering maiden Martha reminded Mary to make meals, but the marvelous Master mattered more. [Martha made meals, but to Mary the Master mattered more.]
   - Mary listened, laughed, or leered?
   - Mary chose to spend time with Jesus, listening to Him instead of working busily to feed Him. Was she being lazy or wise? Why? (Luke 10:38–42).
   - When is it more important to be still than busy—even busy helping others?

The Bible is full of great examples of people to learn from. Qualities such as the ones these characters showed are qualities you can build in your own lives. Try making up tongue twisters about other Bible characters and what you can learn from them.

Listen Carefully

Easy. Trips about 15 minutes. All ages.

Play a game of "Mommy or Daddy says," in the spirit of "Simon says." For example, "*Mommy says* put your hands on your head. *Mommy says* touch your nose to your knee. *Mommy says* sing 'Mary Had a Little Lamb.' Touch your finger to your nose—Aah, *Mommy* didn't say to do it!"

- How can you listen just as carefully to what God is saying to you? What negative consequences happened in the Bible when people didn't do as God told them to? (For example, consider Jonah, Eve, Cain, and others.)
- In what ways do you listen and respond well?

Dozens of Praises

Easy. Any length trip. All ages. Improves the atmosphere in the car.

Work together or in teams to find words of praise or affirmation on the signs and vehicles around you. When a good adjective or complement is found, each person on the team uses the word in a sentence that builds up someone else in the car. Younger children (3–6 years) will have trouble finding words but can certainly use the words in a sentence. If the word is unfamiliar to them, explain it simply.

For example, look for words like *good, great, fantastic, wonderful, awesome*. Players follow with phrases such as, "Mom is a *fantastic* cook!" or "Jasmine did an *awesome* job being helpful today!"

- How can you remember to praise each other more?
- Talk with your children about how praise makes them feel. For example, ask, "Do you like it when I tell you that you did a great job cleaning your room?" or "When you heard me tell Grandma that you brought me breakfast in bed for Mother's Day, how did you feel?"

Billboards to Parables

Moderate. Trips 30 minutes or longer. Best for 7–10 years, but younger children may wish to try. Best where signs abound, on highways or in the city.

Parables are stories that teach a principle or lesson. Jesus often taught using parables.

Below are some sample parable titles that you and your family can use to create your own parables from billboards and your imagination. Each title has a suggested "lesson" or topic it can be used to teach. Use it or choose your own. The stories should be fun and creative, but they need to teach the lesson. Here's how:

1. Read aloud one of the titles.
2. Have someone suggest a silly thing from a sign or vehicle to fill in the [item from billboard] slot in the title. For instance, "The [Racecar] That Learned to Forgive" or "The Lost [Can of Coke™]." If everyone agrees on the title, begin the story.
3. The person who thought of the title starts the story by providing the first one to three sentences. For example, "Roland Racecar was spinning along well when Tommy Turbo cut him off and forced him off the track . . ."
4. Everyone adds to the story until it is told and the lesson is taught. Don't be afraid to get silly as long as the point of the lesson is made.

Here are sample titles to get you going:
- "The [item from billboard] That Learned to Forgive" (teach forgiveness)
- "The Lost [item from billboard]" (teach God's care)
- "The [item from billboard] Who Could Not Tell a Lie" (teach honesty)
- "The Embarrassed [item from billboard]" (teach how to respond well in difficult situations)
- "The Parable of the Rude [item from billboard]" (teach respect)
- "The Joyful [item from billboard]" (teach joy or gratitude)
- "The [item from billboard] Who Hated to Study" (teach diligence)
- "How [item from billboard] Learned to Be Kind" (teach kindness)
- "The [item from billboard] Who Thought He Knew It All" (teach humility and willingness to learn)
- "The [item from billboard] Who Couldn't Smile" (teach choosing to be positive)

Make up your own titles from scratch once you've got the hang of it.

Watch Where You're Going*

Easy to Moderate. Trips 30 to 45 minutes. Ages 7–10.
Have a map handy.

Give your children a map and ask them to find the silliest names on the map and the most direct route between where you are (or home) and there. Once they determine the route, ask them how much out of the way it would be to go a ridiculously different route instead. Let them count miles.

Now, talk about what would happen if you got rid of the map and tried to drive to the silly location without looking at the road directions. You would just drive around until you found it, right? How long might that take? Might you NEVER find it?

- How important is it to know where you're headed?
- How important is it to know how to get there?
- How are your lives like the map?
- Describe the life of someone who knows where he or she is going and how to get there.
- Describe the life of someone who knows where he or she wants to end up but is a little mixed-up and off course. What can a person do in this case?

Word Pictures

Easy. Any length trip. All ages.

Use your imagination and things you see around you to make up word pictures that help you visualize a concept. Use concepts from the following list or add your own: heaven, family of God, hope, guilt, freedom, sin, serving, obeying, believing, witnessing, praying, grace, peace, clean heart, blessings, thankfulness, truthfulness, patience, gladness, joy, love, contentment, wisdom.

For example, let's say the concept is "heaven." Players look around for something they can use to begin to describe one concept of heaven. Someone may see a McDonald's and say, "*Heaven* is like a McDonalds' playland with free food and a live orchestra." Other players can then build on that comment by looking for other word pictures about heaven.

For the concept of hope someone might say, "*Hope* is seeing the Dairy Queen sign in the middle of the Sahara Desert." Then someone else makes up something that also describes hope. When one concept is exhausted, move on to a different one.

Use players' statements as jumping off points to talk about those concepts. If a player's statement shows that he or she doesn't understand the concept, this is a great time to clarify it for him or her.

Pig Latin Fun

Easy. Trips about 15 minutes. All ages

If your children have not already learned how to speak Pig Latin, explain how this fun twist on words works: The first consonant of a word is removed and added to the end of the word with the addition of the sound "ay." Barnabas becomes "ArnabasBay," Caesar becomes "AesarSay." When a name begins with a vowel, such as Adam, just add "ay" to the end, thus "Adamay."

Ask each child to make up a new Bible name in Pig Latin within 10 seconds. When a player can't think of one or messes up, he or she is out. This can also be played with Bible objects, objects in the car, extended family names, and so on.

- To play this game correctly, you have to keep focused, remember the rules, think before you speak, and try hard to be consistent. Use this game to point out how God wants you to live your lives as consistently as possible.
- How can you learn to be more consistent with your actions, words, and the ways you spend your time?

Whistle If You Can*

Easy. Trips about 15 minutes. Anyone who can whistle.

Take along some plain crackers (5–6 per person). Have a contest to see who can eat his or her crackers quickly and be the first to whistle "Jesus Loves Me." Ready. Set. Go!

- Could you whistle right away? What had to happen before you could whistle?
- If whistling is compared to being truthful, what things can make it difficult to tell the truth, just like the crackers made it difficult to whistle (such as attitudes, thoughts, or feelings)?
- Why is it important to tell the truth? What benefits are there?

"Truthful lips endure forever, but a lying tongue lasts only a moment" (Proverbs 12:19).

Kingdomly Top Five Lists

Easy. Any length trip. All ages. Great for kids who love to joke around.

Read these for a humorous look at life's dilemmas. See what additions you can make to finish the lists. Make the #1 answer a truly good reason, such as "Your Mom told you your room is a mess and you want to surprise her by doing something about it before she asks you to!" If kids have trouble coming up with the serious "good reason," use the opportunity to discuss the topic and instill your values in them.

TOP FIVE WAYS TO KNOW IT'S TIME TO CLEAN UP YOUR ROOM!

5. You can't remember what color your carpet is.
4.
3.
2.

And the #1 way to know it's time to clean up your room is:
1.

TOP FIVE THINGS BIBLICAL KIDS MIGHT HAVE SAID TO THEIR MOMS

5. The Philistines are making fun of me, Mom. Any chance I can get a haircut?
4.
3.
2.

And the #1 answer that biblical kids might have said to their Moms is:
1.

TOP FIVE REASONS TO CLOSE YOUR EYES DURING PRAYER

5. So you can try to forget that Dad is blessing the liver and onions.
4.
3.
2.

And the #1 reason to close your eyes during prayer is:
1.

Have some fun making up your own Kingdomly Top Five Lists. Some more ideas are:

- Top Five Ways to Raise Money for Your Church
- Top Five Things Kids Say Before School in the Morning
- Top Five Ways to Be Placed on the Prayer List at Church
- Top Five Excuses for Not Doing Chores
- Top Five Exercises for Lazy Families
- Top Five Ways to Watch Less Television

This is a fun exercise in seeing the humor in everyday situations. Christians can laugh at themselves, too!

Coin Hide[*]

Easy. Trips about 30 minutes. All ages.

(Hide from 5 to 10 coins per child in the car—in compartments, under the mat, or wherever your kids will have the opportunity to find them from their seats with their seatbelts on.)

When you are on your way, tell your children that they are to find hidden coins, but don't tell them how many. They are to close their eyes and keep them shut as they try to find the coins by feeling around. After a time, offer clues to help them know where to "look." If you notice someone is not being honest about keeping his or her eyes shut, you will have to disqualify him or her. The winner is the one who keeps his or her eyes closed and successfully finds the allotted number of coins.

- Talk about the process. What made finding the coins easier? (More information.)
- In the same way, you can judge whether something is right or wrong by having more information about it. This information can be found in the Bible.

Church Signs

Hard. Any length trip. Best suited to older children (7 years and up) because it can be tough. However, some little ones have creative thoughts to share, too.

Have you seen church signs with humorous messages that get you thinking? Here are some actual church sign messages for you to read. Briefly talk about what you think each one means before moving on.

1. People are like tea bags . . . you have to put them in hot water before you know how strong they are.
2. God so loved the world that He did not send a committee.
3. When down in the mouth, remember Jonah. He came out all right.
4. Fight truth decay—study the Bible daily.
5. If you're headed in the wrong direction, God allows U-turns.
6. This is a C–H–*space*–*space*–C–H. What is missing?
7. In the dark? Follow the S–O–N.

Now have fun making up messages for church signs as a family, or spotting new ones while you drive. For example, fill in the blanks to these to get started. You can make sentences that rhyme or that just state something truthful in an unusual way:

1. If you're always _____ (running late/tired and grumpy . . .), check your _____ (batteries/energy source . . .).
2. Think you're in a _____ (jam/pickle/hard place . . .)? Jesus is the _____ (Bread/Rock . . .).
3. People are like _____ (pizza/ice cream/eggs). When the temperature changes, they often _____ (sizzle/melt/boil . . .).
4. Almost on empty? _____.
5. When your number is dialed, _____ the call.

Read My Lips

Easy. Any length trip. All ages. Not an appropriate game for the driver to participate in.

How good are your children at reading lips? You need two or more players who are able to see each other well, preferably sitting in the same bench seat.

Play this game by mouthing the words to short well-known phrases that:

1. Have been spoken in your home, but aren't so great, such as, "Get off my back," "Take a hike," "No way," "Liar, liar, pants on fire."
2. Would be nice to hear more often at your house, such as, "I love you," or perhaps, "Way to go!" "Thank you very much," or "Great job."

The first person mouths the phrase once, slowly and carefully, to see if the partner can read lips and repeat aloud what was mouthed. Allow up to three chances for that phrase to be mouthed before the turn is proclaimed over and the answer given. Then the other person has a chance to mouth a phrase, repeating it up to three times.

After each phrase is guessed, ask questions like:
- How would you feel if that were said more often at our house?
- How can your words affect other people?
- Do you want our home to be a safe place, where you feel loved and accepted—or a place where we criticize one another and argue? Why?

God's Word says, "May the words of my mouth and the meditation of my heart be pleasing in your sight, O LORD" (Psalm 19:14).

Cooperation Challenge*

Easy. Any length trip. All ages. Encourages cooperative interaction between siblings, especially an older and a younger child.

This activity requires a piece of paper for folding, and two people sitting beside one another in the vehicle to work as a team. (If you have two sets of partners, you can have a competition to see which team completes the task first.) The person on the right supplies the right hand and the person on the left supplies the left hand. The other hands are placed behind backs to keep them out of the way. The two partners work together to make an airplane, hat, or boat from the piece of paper—whatever they are familiar with folding. How well can they cooperate to accomplish the task? They might wish to try tying a shoe or braiding a doll's hair. Have them attempt anything you can think of that would be fun to do with one hand each from two people.
- Why is cooperating with others important?
- What happens when you try to accomplish something with another person but you don't work together well? Is it more fun to work toward the same goal or to fight?
- What would not get done at your house if you didn't have any cooperation?
- What difference does talking things out make to how well you work together?

Have fun with it. The Bible says in Ephesians 4:2: "Be patient, bearing with one another in love."

Jaw Droppers

Easy. Any length trip. All ages. Not an appropriate game for the driver to participate in.

Players compete with their bodies and facial gestures. A parent or the oldest passenger chooses the winner of the following contests.

- The saddest looking face.
- The best pouty face.
- The happiest face.
- The most surprised face.
- Expressions of awe or approval. (For example, thumbs up, nods, round "wow!" mouths.)
- Now, have contestants limber up their jaws a bit. Who can drop their jaw the farthest?
- When do you think people usually drop their jaws? (Amazement, awe, . . .). God is able to do and fix anything. You can drop your jaws in amazement at His abilities.
- Now, see who can make the best "God is awesome" face and gestures.

    Give rewards or cheers for the best faces.

Look Up

Easy. Trips of 30 minutes or longer. All ages. Play this game on a day with lots of fluffy clouds in the sky.

Look out of the window at the clouds for a few minutes. Use your imagination to see what types of shapes you can see in the cloud formations. Who can spot the following shapes first?

1. Animal
2. Family member's profile
3. Piece of candy
4. Ice cream cone
5. Other food item
6. Dinosaur
7. Tool
8. Piece of furniture

- What are clouds good for? For example, can they help you make a decision? Exodus 13:21 (emphasis added) tells how God led the Israelites when they didn't know which direction to go. "By day the LORD went ahead of them i*n a pillar of cloud* to guide them on their way and by night in a pillar of fire to give them light." God gave the people a huge cloud to follow, so they knew where to go!
- Point to a cloud in the sky. Where would you end up if you followed it?
- Help your children understand that God wants to guide them, if they'll let Him. He probably won't use a cloud, but He can guide their thoughts, hearts, and lives if they trust Him and ask Him to. Talk about ways God has guided members of your family.

Gotta Study It!*

Moderate. Any length trip. Ages 7–10. Make sure that your vehicle manual is in the vehicle.

What is a driver supposed to do if a warning light comes on in the vehicle? Or what should he or she do if the dashboard lights go out? (See if you can get one of the children to figure out that they should look in the manual. Give a prize to the first child who does.)
- How does looking in the manual help?
- Talk about some warning lights that may come on in your life (depression, temptation, bad dreams, worry, etc.).
- When warning lights appear in your life, where will you turn for help and direction?

What Was That?*

Easy. Trips of 45 minutes or longer. All ages.

Everyone who is playing will need a piece of paper and a pen or pencil. Now empty out the contents of either a glove compartment or a purse (with permission!!). All the players examine the objects for a brief period of time. The objects are then covered up or quickly put back in their rightful places. Players write down every object they can remember in one minute. See who remembers the most objects.

If you have young players who would enjoy playing this verbally, simply see who can call out the most items.

- Everyone forgets things sometimes. What are some things you tend to forget (from the mundane—keys—to the sublime—God is all-powerful)?
- The Bible says that God's Spirit will help you to remember things about Jesus that you have learned. What are a few things about Jesus you want to be able to remember?
- You can depend on God to help you.

Knees, Knees

Easy. Any length trip. All ages.

The first thing you have to do for this game is to get the rhythm going with all the players in the vehicle. Together (but not too loud to frazzle Mom or Dad), everybody slaps both of their hands on their knees two times in a row, then snaps their right middle finger, then their left middle finger:

Knees (one), knees (two), right snap (three), left snap (four)—continuing over and over. Get the rhythm going together at a fairly slow pace so players can say a few words in rhythm with the snaps. Now, in this game, *no words are said on the knees, knees.* But on the right snap and left snap players take turns going around the circle (or carload), calling out ways to serve others or God.

For example:

Knees (one), knees (two), ("take-out-the"), ("trash").
Knees (one), knees (two), ("clean-the"), ("garage").
Knees (one), knees (two), ("go-to"), ("church").

This is a quick-thinking game. When someone messes up by not thinking of something on time, saying something that has nothing to do with serving, or getting off the rhythm, that person has a point against him or her. (The winner will be the one with the lowest points.) After each mistake, start again. Have fun playing as long as you want and seeing how creatively you can think about being a servant.

For added challenge, speed up the rhythm.

Lighter Than Air

Easy. Trips about 15 minutes. All ages.

Have your children put both hands, palm side down, underneath their legs. In other words, each arm is placed beside the outside of each leg, hands slipped under the legs, palms down. Now, using a good deal of effort, have the children pull up against the force of their legs with their hands and maintain this muscle tension for at least 40 seconds. Now have them release their hands and lean forward enough so that their arms drop freely in front of the seat. Have them let their arms dangle and see what happens.

The children worked hard for 40 seconds or so, and now their arms just want to fly when the resistance is released!

- In the Christian life, what things (like your legs) can keep you from soaring?
- Let the "lighter than air" trick help you remember to give your problems to God. What can you give Him now?

Funny Phrases

Moderate. Trips about 30 minutes. All ages.

Take any of the suggested words below and separate the letters. Use each letter to form a new word, so that when the words are said in the correct sequence you have a memorable phrase that goes with the meaning of the word. Younger children will need help, but after doing a couple, they will probably catch on.

For example, HELP could be made into the phrase, Hands Employed Loving People.

Word list: LOVE, CARE, HOPE, GOOD, PURE, SURE

If someone doubts the phrase, have the child explain how it describes the meaning of that word.

Other fun words to use include family names, pet names, and favorite things.

Newspaper Hunt*

Hard. Trips of one hour or longer. Ages 7 and up with a grade three or four reading level.

Find a section of the newspaper that doesn't have objectionable content and that your children can handle reading. Give each child his or her own section and a pen or highlighter to make marks. Challenge the children to search through their paper and circle or highlight all the times they read about something done that was a *good example* to others. For instance, a fireman rescued a little boy from a raging fire, a sports figure complimented the opposing team on a game well played, volunteers helped rebuild a storm-devastated community.

Give the children 10 minutes. Have them read their examples to you and discuss why they thought they were worth highlighting.

Holiday Hunt

Easy. Short trips across town during seasonal holidays. All ages.

Use the various seasonal holiday symbols that people display in yards or on houses to have a fun counting game. On your way to your destination, see how many of the items you can find.

Some suggestions are given of ways that you can tie the game in to a value you may wish to talk about.

1. Christmas: Count wreaths. [God's love is continuous, like a circle.]
2. Valentine's Day: Count hearts on signs or look for the word "love." [Ways you can give love to each other.]
3. St. Patrick's Day: Count green cars or trucks or vans or whatever. [Green with envy? Let's talk about it.]
4. April Fool's Day: Look for people doing foolish things such as speeding, driving funny because of talking on the cell phone, etc. [Be wise.]
5. Easter: Look for crosses. [Forgive as Christ has forgiven us.]
6. Independence Day: Count flags. [Don't be ashamed of who you are in Christ.]
7. Labor Day: Count people that you see laboring (at work). [Responsibility.]

8. Halloween (or other fall day): Count pumpkins. [The effects of a cheerful face.]
9. Thanksgiving: Count white mailboxes, since many people send notes of thanks and appreciation through the mail. [Ways to give thanks to the Lord.]

Bible Story Mix-up*

Moderate. Trips of one hour or longer. Ages 7 and up. Can be played with just two people, but a larger carload is fun for this game. You'll need paper and pens or pencils.

First you'll need a piece of paper and a pencil or pen for every person playing (excluding the driver). Players think of a Bible story but don't tell anyone what it is. Players write *who* they are thinking of at the top of their pages, and then turn the top edge of the paper down to cover the writing. Everyone passes their paper to the person on their left.

Without looking at what the other person wrote, everyone writes *what* the character did in the story they're thinking about, then folds down the edge to cover up what they've written. The papers are then handed on to the next person on the left, who writes *when* their character did something. This pattern continues, completing *who*, *what*, *when*, *where*, *how*, and *why*. When those six elements have been completed, the papers are unfolded and the mixed-up elements are read as stories for some laughs.

• Talk about some of the qualities your chosen Bible characters had that are admirable or desirable for your children to learn from.

MUSIC/MEDIA FUN

Radio Jump

Moderate. Any length trip. All ages.

Turn on the radio and scan the channels, listening to each for a few seconds. Have your children call out the style of the music to the best of their ability. Perhaps they will not be able to identify a particular style for some stations. Some stations will have talking going on, in which case you can just jump to the next station.

- How do the various styles affect your emotions?
- Are there some styles it would be better not to listen to? Why or why not?

Next, play the same game again, but instead of listening for the style of music, have the children try to hear a message from the song if they can identify it within those few seconds. (Sample messages could include sadness, love, anger, hurt, or just plain music.)

- Which of those messages are ones you think God would approve of? Why?
- Which messages are true?
- How should you decide what to listen to?

My Word*

Easy. Trips of more than 30 minutes. All ages.

1. Play a story on tape or listen to an adventure on the radio. However, prior to starting to listen to the story, have each child pick a word that he or she thinks might come up in the story, such as "friend" or "love." See who can call out "My Word" the most often in the story when his or her word is said.
2. Alternatively, you could stop the tapes at certain points and ask, "What should (name a character) do next? Why?"

Then start the tape and see what the character does.

- Pause the tape again and ask how the suggested choice was better or worse than what the character did. Why?

Try *Adventures in Odyssey!* tapes. They are specifically designed to dramatize Christian values using characters your children can relate to. They and other such tapes can lead to great discussions. (You might find these in your church or local public library. Call 1-800-A-FAMILY for more information or check out the *Adventures in Odyssey* Web site at www.adventuresinodyssey.org. The *Adventures in Odyssey* adventures are also often broadcast over the radio on Christian stations. On the same Web site you can enter your zip code to find out exactly when *Adventures in Odyssey* is broadcast in your area. This might help you plan when to take your half-hour drive this Saturday.)

Keep the Faith*

Moderate. Any length trip. All ages.

Either play a Christian music tape or CD or find a Christian radio station that is playing music. Challenge the children to listen closely to the words of the song being sung. Can they identify anything said in the song that can help them "keep the faith"? For instance, phrases like "It's time to praise the Lord," "Gotta keep your eyes on Jesus," "Why should I worry?" and "Jesus will still be there" are all phrases that can be said either to yourself or to someone else as a reminder to be faithful to God.

As an alternate, have children write down the phrases that they hear. At the end of the drive, see who has the most "keep the faith" phrases written down.

It's All in a Word

Easy. Any length trip. All ages. Good for anyone who likes songs.

Use the following list of words to get your children started for this game. One child calls out a word and challenges the others to think of a song with that word in it. Whoever thinks of a song sings the phrase that includes the word. Sometimes a word may completely stump everyone. (Score one for the invisible man, in that case.)

Words to get you started: follow, turn, run, walk, stop, sing, listen, pray, fall, fear, honesty, truth, right, wrong, trust, live, watch, up, down, see, hear, feel, touch, taste, sweet, song, music, face, cross.

Backseat Clap and Rap

Easy. Any length trip. All ages. Gets the children interacting and having fun.

Have the children make up a short rhyming ditty about your family or about where you're headed in the car right now. Use the following examples to get your children going.

1. We're headed to the _____, my dad and me.
   We're gonna eat _____ and _____, you see.
   And when the _____ is over, it's plain to see
   We'll be laughin' and a cryin' with _____ on our knees.

2. Yes, we like our dad. He is really great.
   Except he likes to _____.
   Our mom, we think is just the best.
   Even when she _____.

3. We love going to church, that's no lie.
   It makes a dull day just turn out _____.
   First thing we'll do is _____.
   After that we _____.

4. I just can't wait to eat some pie.
   The thought makes me _____ and _____.
   My stomach's _____ fit to kill.
   Soon my longing will be _____.

Perhaps you are familiar with some clapping games where children face a partner and clap on their own knees, clap their hands together, and then clap their partners' hands in differing arrangements. It's a bit more challenging in the car since your children can't face each other, but you can suggest adding some raps and claps to the ditty. Go for it and have some fun.

Some of the possible clapping styles that can be used are clapping both hands on the child's own knees; clapping his or her own hands together; clapping the child's outside hand with his or her partner's outside hand (like a high five); clapping the back of his or her inside hand and the back of the partner's inside hand together (gently—knuckles colliding!); circling his or her inside hand with the partner's inside hand to clap them together; snapping fingers; clapping his or her partner's knee.

- Talk about how your family works. What do you like about it or don't you like about it? Can you put that into a ditty?
- What's the rhythm at your house? Frantic, just right, lazy? Talk about it.

Next, turn on the CD or tape player to some music that you can all enjoy. Continue the clap and raps to the music.

The Singing Bible*

Easy. Any length trip, but best for longer ones. All ages.

Listen to *The Singing Bible* tapes—a great resource for learning and having fun with music. *The Singing Bible* is an action-packed audio musical that takes kids through the Bible in 51 songs and four acts (four tapes). (Available at Christian bookstores or through Focus on the Family.)

Because music is such a great teaching tool, these tapes are a great investment for your kids. They help children get a grasp of a biblical timeline, while instilling God's truth in their hearts.

Make sure you ask questions about the songs to open up conversations to increase your children's understanding—and perhaps Mom and Dad's as well.

Here are some ways to question your kids about songs you've all just listened to:

1. Repeat a memorable phrase from the song, leaving one word blank for the children to fill in—see if they've been listening to the words.
2. Without looking at the tape insert ask, "What do you think a good title for that song might be?" Then check it out to see how close it is to the actual title.
3. Ask for one thing the song mentioned that made your children think about something new.
4. What was the main point or message of the song?
5. If the song mentions a number of any kind (for example, Joseph had ELEVEN brothers; God sent TEN plagues), ask, "Did you hear any numbers in that song? Okay, what was

the number and what did it refer to?" (Eleven brothers, ten plagues.)

6. Another way to use the tapes is to listen to one entire tape before asking questions about which events came before other events. How did one event lead into or affect another event? This is helpful to get the timeline straight in their heads. Many biblical events will make more sense to your children when they can place them within a mental time frame.

Humble Harmonies*

Easy. Trips of 15 minutes and up. Ages 3–10. This goofy activity is good for overactive bodies.

Needed: A box of flex-straws (the straws that bend at one end) or at least one flex-straw for each participant.

For a totally crazy musical experience, hand each child a flex-straw. The straws are bent and the short side placed inside clothing into the person's armpit. Participants blow into the other end, making a unique, perhaps annoying, human trombone sound. See if kids can work together to toot a song. Or play some music over the radio and blow along.

Dispose of the straws after use!

- Almost anything can be used to make music. Name some crazy musical instruments (like grass, spoons, noisy stomachs . . .).
- How can you make unexpected music by turning an unpleasant situation into a "song" or a positive experience?

Musical Hot Potato*

Easy. Any length trip. All ages.

This game is a cross between Hot Potato and Musical Chairs. Use a beanbag or a sock rolled into a knot for the potato. Your children should all be in the back of the vehicle so that the driver doesn't get whacked by accident. The goal is to pass the "potato" quickly between children while the music is playing. When the music stops, whoever is left holding the potato gets a point against him or her—unless someone laughs or makes fun of the person caught with the potato. Then *that* person gets a point against him or her instead. The winner will be the one with the lowest number of points.

Encourage your kids to pour on the sympathy/encouragement to the person who gets caught with the potato each time. If any of the encouragements are so poured on and silly like, "Oh, you poor, poor thing. I'm SO sorry that the hot potato landed in your lovely lap. I hope it doesn't burn you," that they make Mom or Dad laugh out loud, then that silly person gets a point deducted from their score. So go ahead and be silly.

Okay, Mom or Dad, turn on the tape or CD music. Turn the mute button off and on as you wish.

- Don't think too highly of yourself. When you are critical of others' mistakes, you've forgotten how often you blow it yourself. What are some things others do that bother you, yet you do them too?
- Everyone makes mistakes and gets caught holding the "potato" sometimes. Think of some ways you can be nice to others when they make mistakes. (For example, help them clean up the mess . . .)

Do You Remember?*

Moderate. Any length trip. All ages.

If you have a tape player in your vehicle, don't miss the opportunity available through many local libraries to check out books on tape. Find some classic children's novels, such as *Charlotte's Web*, *Swiss Family Robinson*, or *Charlie and the Chocolate Factory*. These tapes can be played while you drive. Your children will listen, learn, and look forward to getting back into the vehicle to hear what happens next. Further reinforce listening skills by following up with questions about what has been said on the tape. See how well your children remember the details. Or, for a scarier scenario, have the children ask *you* questions! Sometimes adults have a harder time remembering the details than children do.

Here are some general questions you can use to help your children interact with and apply what they are hearing.

- What lessons are the characters in this story learning?
- What could they have done differently?
- What would you have done? Why?

Some classic children's stories may introduce your children to ideas or language that you object to. These are teachable moments. Use them to talk about and teach your values to your children.

MISSION: ROLE-PLAY

In this section your children are given a situation with some kind of conflict or choice in it. Their mission, should they choose to accept it, is to choose roles and act out the situation to achieve the desired end result. (Sample desired results are provided.) Actors are encouraged to have fun and be creative! There are many ways to achieve the same result. If they want, they can switch roles to come up with alternate ways to make the right choice. Give hints to stumped actors to help them identify with their character. Younger children will need more direction and cues, but they can understand the principle and might come up with unique approaches.

Broken Elbows

Easy. Trips longer than 20 minutes. All ages.

There is a tree in the playground at school that is super cool to climb. Last week when Billy climbed up to the top branches, a small limb broke and he fell and broke his arm. It could have been a lot worse. Billy is now daring Josh to go as high as he did—or else Josh is a chicken.

(Someone be Billy. Someone be Josh. Others can play the parts of other kids. Start out on the ground by the tree.)

Desired end result: Use the wisdom learned from someone else's mistake and don't repeat the same mistake just to be "cool."

Broken Windows

Easy. Trips longer than 20 minutes. All ages.

The neighbor's window is found broken. He jumps to the conclusion that a certain kid who is often getting in trouble did it. Sam knows who did it, and it wasn't that kid. The kid being accused is mean to Sam and the other kids all the time.

(Someone be Sam. Someone be the neighbor man. Someone be the kid being accused. Start out with the neighbor accusing the boy.)

Desired end result: The accused kid learns to treat others correctly by seeing how Sam stood up for him and hearing Sam tell the neighbor what he knew. He and Sam even end up as friends.

Funeral Woes

Hard. Trips longer than 20 minutes. All ages.

With her parents, Jill has to attend a funeral for someone that she didn't even know. How boring can that be?

(Someone be Jill, someone be one or both parents, others can be guests at the funeral. Start out as Jill arrives at the funeral.)

Desired end result: Jill's parents tell her over pizza later that they heard lots of compliments on her attitude that day.

Biblical Replay

Moderate. Trips longer than 20 minutes. All ages.

Have your children pick one or more of the following Bible stories to "replay" with a different end. They should choose people to play the different characters in the story and act out the situations with words. Discuss why the actors chose to play their roles the way they did. Think of other examples to act out as well. If children are not familiar with the story, you or an older child can explain it or read it from the Bible.

- What might have happened if, instead of hiding, Adam and Eve had gone to God and confessed what they had done? (Genesis 3.) Act it out. (Assign children to be Adam, Eve, God, and the serpent.)
- Remember the story about Ananias and Sapphira selling some land and lying about the amount to the apostles? They said

that the amount they laid at the apostles' feet was the entire amount when they had really kept back some for themselves. What would have happened differently if they had been honest? (Acts 5:1–11.) Act it out. (Assign children to be Ananias, Sapphira, Peter, and the person who bought the land.)

- Peter denied Jesus three times just as Jesus had predicted. What might have happened if he had told the truth? (Luke 22:54–62.) Act it out. (Assign children to be Peter, a woman in the courtyard who accuses Peter, other bystanders, and the rooster.)

Please Don't Brag

Easy. Trips longer than 20 minutes. All ages.

Ian has a friend up the street he likes to play with most of the time. The problem is that the friend, Josh, occasionally brags about playing ball better than Ian, or that his dad makes more money than Ian's dad, or that he gets more allowance than Ian does, and so on. It irritates Ian. Play out the interactions and outcome between the two friends.

(Assign a child to be Josh and a child to be Ian. Switch roles for a new approach.)

Desired end result: The boys stay friends.

Decisions, Decisions

Moderate. Trips longer than 20 minutes. All ages.

Discuss the following questions with your children before having them do the role-play:

- How do you decide what flavor of ice cream cone you want when you go to the ice cream shop? Discuss everyone's favorite flavors. Point out that some choices are just preferences.
- How do you make a decision if someone asks you to do something that you know is wrong? God's Word makes some decisions clear.

Role-play: Mom and Dad are in the middle of a huge decision regarding a new job that Dad has just been offered in another part of the world. Everyone plays him- or herself and acts like this job really is a consideration. Let your imaginations go as you work through making a big decision like this.

Desired outcome: There is unity in the family and you sense God's peace about the decision.

- How do you go about making a decision like this one?
- Some decisions are made with much prayer and trust in God to direct. You still need to consider all the pros and cons. Ultimately your lives are in God's hands and you need to trust Him to give you wisdom. Is it always easy to do? Why or why not?

How Embarrassing!

Easy. Trips longer than 20 minutes. All ages.

For this role-play, have one child think of something that he or she does really well. Now have the child act out a situation where he or she is doing that special something—but he really goofs this time. What happens?

(Assign other children in the car to be observers who react in various ways to the child's goof. The child acts out how he or she would respond to the observers' responses. For example, how would he or she act if the observer laughed? Made fun of him or her? Ignored him or her? Was sympathetic? Act out each scenario.)

Desired end result: The child doesn't think of him- or herself too highly and reacts with a humble spirit.

Lost Again

Easy. Trips longer than 20 minutes. All ages.

Before doing this role-play, have a little fun getting into the subject matter by coming up with fictitious book titles and why the books were lost. Some examples: *Everything Kids Should Know About Returning Library Books* (excuse: it was too small to find), *The Big Book of Lame Excuses* (excuse: the dog ate it), *The Book of Mother's Wisdom* (excuse: it was too big to carry).

A library book is lost. Each child takes a role to play and talks through this situation.

(Assign a librarian, the borrower, a friend—maybe even the book.)

Desired end result: Some steps are taken to keep the problem from happening again.

LET'S PRETEND

This section provides some pretend situations and stories, but they're all missing parts. The children's job is to fill in the missing pieces to see how the situation or story turns out. Encourage them to be as crazy and creative as they want. When they're done, talk about the story using the questions provided or some of your own. They can then redo the story taking it in a different direction to see what happens.

For younger children, you could start the various stories off by choosing a situation they would be familiar with or can imagine easily.

Pickup Mix-up

Easy. Trips longer than 20 minutes. All ages. Note: Someone other than the driver needs to read the story.

• Kids provide the information asked for in the parentheses.

Pretend your mom had asked (someone you know) to pick you up after (an activity—ballet, basketball, . . .) but they forgot. You are there all by yourself, waiting at the (where? curb, roadside . . .). You feel (how?). Then a stranger offers you (what?). You think the right thing to do is (what?). You decide to (what?). Later, when your mom finds out what happened, she (what?). You feel (how?) about the way things turned out.

Time Travel

Moderate. Trips longer than 20 minutes. All ages. Note: Someone other than the driver needs to read the story.

• Ask your children to fill in the blanks as the story is read, getting as silly as they want. The story is started for them with a couple of options. Keep going along one of those lines or choose a different direction.

• Add details to each "blank." For example: What would doing _____ be like? What tools would they need? What would they be wearing? Encourage them to let their imaginations go wild.

- When they're finished with the story, answer the questions following it to see how they did.

Let's pretend—you're traveling back in time to _____ (e.g., A.D. 1400, the time of knights in shining armor, . . .). This is particularly cool because _____ (you always wanted to be a damsel in distress, you're an old war-horse anyway, . . .). You want to spend your day _____ (practicing jousting, digging a moat, . . .). Things just start to get fun when, all of a sudden, an old _____ (horse, pig, woman, knight, . . .) has an accident beside the _____ (river, castle, trough, outhouse, . . .). (Describe what happened—make it very sad.) You really don't want to _____, but your heart _____. You react by _____. The old _____ responds (how? doing and saying what? . . .). On your way back to the present you think that you did the (best/worst) thing by _____ because _____.

- Compassion describes how someone feels when he or she sees the distress of others and wants to help. In the story, did the children feel compassion for the old _____ or not? Why?
- If the story didn't evoke feelings of compassion, try it again with new fill-in-the-blanks to develop a story that displays compassion.

Angels on Guard

Easy. Trips longer than 20 minutes. All ages. Note: Someone other than the driver needs to read the story.

Let's pretend—you see an angel guarding you at _____ (preschool, school, or sports practice, . . .). Surprisingly, the angel is wearing a funny _____ (extra set of wings, belt, backpack, . . .). Your first reaction is _____. The angel says, "I'm here to help you with _____." You ask the angel to _____. All of a sudden you hear the loudest _____ (scream, thunder, name, drill, music, . . .) and _____ (the building, your pants, . . .) begin falling faster than anything! The best thing you can think to do is _____. You can put your trust in God by _____.

- The way the story worked out, did the children trust God? Why or why not?
- If the story was serious, try a humorous one or vice versa. Try a different scenario and follow it through the blanks.
- Ask your passengers if they can share a story from their lives in which they trusted God. What happened?

Finders Keepers

Hard. Trips longer than 20 minutes. All ages. Note: Someone other than the driver needs to read the story.

Let's pretend—you found a hidden box of money under the _____ (bathroom floor, couch, garage, . . .) in _____ (the neighbor's, your, your enemy's, . . .) house. The box looked like _____ (a chicken, a pirate's chest, a library book, . . .). You have never seen a box so _____ (dirty, small, decorated, . . .) before. There is money inside! There is also a note that says "_____" (something you should do with the money). You think about what you could do with _____ dollars! You could spend the money on _____ or do what the note said. Thinking about using the money is _____. Your choices of what to do now are to _____ or _____. You feel the right thing to do is _____ because _____.

- Why is doing what is right sometimes difficult?
- What might be a surprising reward in the above situation?
- Is it always clear what is right or wrong? Why or why not?
- If you don't feel that the above story got at the issue of right and wrong, try retelling it with the children filling in the blanks differently.

Role Reversal

Easy. Trips longer than 20 minutes. All ages.

In this scenario, the children are the dads or moms. They have five kids, all of them hungry and tired from a day with relatives. (You can play the part of whiny kids). The kids (you) are whining and complaining about being hungry, about being tired of riding in the car, about brothers or sisters bugging them, and so on. It's a long drive home!

One of the parents has $5 in his or her pocket. Ask your children how they, as the parents, would handle dealing with the stress in an appropriate way? Ready to act? Go!

- Is your family ever like this?
- Do your kids have any suggestions for Mom or Dad now that they've thought about how they would react being in your shoes?
- Did they react in a kind way with their "kids?" Why or why not?
- Did you learn anything by experiencing your kids as *your* parents? What?

Squeak and Peek

Easy. Trips longer than 20 minutes. All ages but especially good for ages 3–6. Note: Someone other than the driver needs to read the story.

Let's pretend—you are mice hiding in the _____ when Jesus was born. The animals are talking to each other about _____. Some amazing things you see are _____ and _____. The most interesting visitor in the stable is _____. There is such a _____ feeling surrounding everyone. The ways that you can worship Jesus right now are to _____ and _____. Jesus looks so _____.

Use this as a starting point to talk about worship.
- What leads you into worship?
- Why do you worship God?
- What are qualities in God that deserve worship?

Helping Hand

Moderate. Trips longer than 20 minutes. All ages. Note: Someone other than the driver needs to read the story.

Let's pretend—the doctor has confined your best friend's mother to her bed. She will be lying around for _____ weeks while she gets better. You want to help out by _____ if she will let you. In fact, you would also be able to help by doing _____. Your friend feels _____ about his or her mother. When he or she sees you being a servant by _____, the friend decides to help more, too, by _____. When the

mother sees all the help that she is receiving, she feels
_____. Why?

- Talk about what true servanthood is and how everyone can do it in little and big ways.
- How can you serve each other at home?

Smarty Pants

Easy. Trips longer than 20 minutes. All ages. Note: Someone other than the driver needs to read the story.

Let's pretend—you are so smart for your age that your school has graduated you and sent you off to _____. You feel extremely _____. Your parents tell you that you are _____. Your head starts to swell like a _____ because you think you're pretty _____. Friends start to call you _____. After a while, you wonder why no one wants to _____ with you. Then you decide to change your _____. Instead of bragging about _____, you ask God to help you _____. You feel _____ now that your head is returning to normal size.

- Discuss humility. (Make sure not to give your children the idea that they can't appreciate and enjoy their talents.)
- What's the difference between pride and confidence?

Transformer

Easy. Trips longer than 20 minutes. All ages. Note: Someone other than the driver needs to read the story.

Let's pretend—your car is a _____ (spaceship, submarine, helicopter, . . .). So you are off to _____ (Mars, Mount Everest, the Great Barrier Reef, . . .). There is so much to _____ (explore, eat, paint, . . .). The first thing you want to do is _____. You never thought you would be able to _____, but here you are. It is amazing the way God made _____. The more you explore, the more you appreciate _____.

- Talk about different parts of God's creation and how amazing it is.
- What does it tell you about God?

Get 'Em
Talking

STICKY SITUATIONS

Read each incident and the multiple-choice questions that follow to your children. Children pick the answer that most closely matches what their choice would be. (Feel free to let children make up their own answers too.) Use the follow-up questions to dig a little deeper and to help you share your values. The questions can also help your children articulate their thoughts further.

Children can read the situations to each other, taking turns, or a nondriving parent or adult can read so all the children can answer. In each case, ask the child to explain why he or she chose that answer.

Making Wise Choices

Any length trip. Ages as indicated for each.

"How much better to get wisdom than gold, to choose understanding rather than silver!" (Proverbs 16:16)

1. *(E. All ages.)* You are being disciplined by your father. He said to stay in your room for one hour and study or play until he calls for you. Everyone else is outside playing. The clock is ticking away. It's been close to an hour and a half now. Did he forget? What would you do?
   a. Stay put. You don't want Dad to get upset again.
   b. Stick a white flag out the window. You surrender.
   c. Use the time to write a note of apology to your dad and slide it out under your door.
   d. Go find Dad to see if you can come out now.
   e. Make a huge sign using your sheets to say, "I'm a prisoner. Help!" Hang it out of the window and hope a policeman sees it and rescues you.

   • What do you risk if you come out of your room?
   • If you stay put, and Dad never comes, how will he feel later?

- Do you tend to learn from your mistakes when disciplined? Why or why not?

2. *(M. All ages.)* Tommy wants to light firecrackers behind the barn. Tommy's big brother says it won't hurt anybody and you're a wimp if you won't come along. You've got a knot in your stomach because you've been warned not to play with matches. Your parents would probably never find out. What would you do?
   a. Hold your hand to your ear as if you've just got a message over an ear bug saying your secret agent status has been reactivated. Sorry but you have to go save the world from a mad terrorist.
   b. Go ahead and join in the fun.
   c. Think of a reason to go home early.
   d. Ask your dad to allow you to light firecrackers with Tommy and his brother. Maybe Dad will even help light the matches.
   e. You watch Tommy and his brother but don't help out.
   - Why did you pick the answer you did?
   - What might happen if you chose to disobey?
   - What if you chose answer d., but Dad still says, "No"?

3. *(H. Ages 7 and up.)* Your teacher at school assigns you to read a book that your Sunday school teacher tells you may not be appropriate. What would you do?
   a. Run home as fast as you can so you can read about the weird stuff.
   b. Throw the book away and tell the teacher you lost it.
   c. Talk to your parents about it.
   d. Tell your teacher that there are things in the book that you feel uncomfortable reading. Ask her for an alternate book to read.
   e. Read with the book turned upside-down so that you can tell your teacher you read it but it didn't make sense to you.
   - What is the worst thing that could happen if you talk to your parents or the teacher?
   - What is the worst thing that could happen if you read the book?
   - Proverbs 4:23 says, "Above all else, guard your heart, for it is the wellspring of life." How can you do that?

4. *(M. Ages 11 and up.)* No one is home at your friend's house after school. Your friend asks you to come in and have a drink from the bar. What would you do?
   a. You want to be a good friend, so you politely take a small drink.
   b. You say, "Sure!" and play bartender.
   c. You go home instead of going inside your friend's house.
   d. You suddenly act like you heard thunder and say you have to get home before the judgment of God hits him or her.
   e. You refuse and encourage your friend not to drink either.
   • How important is what your friends say to you? Why?
   • Do you think more about impressing others or being an example to others? Which is harder? Why?

5. *(H. Ages 11 and up.)* At a neighborhood clubhouse in the woods, someone brings out cigarettes and passes them around. Everyone seems to be taking them and lighting up. Then the pack is passed to you. What would you do?
   a. You smile and take two.
   b. You make your knee do a funny jerk and knock the pack of cigarettes onto the ground. You say it's your genetic reflex.
   c. You pretend to have a fainting spell.
   d. You turn and dash for home.
   e. You say, "No thanks. Smoking is bad for you."
   • How could this experience affect your welcome at the clubhouse in future days? Why would that matter?
   • Would you tell anyone what happened? Why or why not?

Loving and Caring for Others

Any length trip. Ages as indicated for each.

"We love because he first loved us." (1 John 4:19)

1. *(M. All ages.)* A neighbor boy your age has been inviting you to his house to play. When you're there he says bad words and lies to his mother. His mother thinks that you may be the troublemaker because the boy blames everything on you when he gets caught. What would you do?
   a. Tell the boy he is a big, ridiculous liar!

    b. Next time you're invited over, laugh in his face.

    c. Next time you're invited over, muster the courage to tell him that you don't like being blamed for things that you didn't do so you're not coming this time.

    d. Go home and talk to your parents about the situation to get their advice.

    e. Paint red spots on your arms and next time he invites you over, show him the spots and tell him you're allergic to bad words and lies so you can't come.

- If you decide to talk to your parents, what do you think they would tell you? Why?
- If you decide to talk to the boy on your own, what would be the best attitude when you tell him why you're not coming?
- What would the best possible outcome be?

2. *(M. All ages.)* On the playground at preschool or school you hear someone calling someone else a bad name. You turn around to see some guys pushing around another kid while saying insulting things about the color of his skin. What would you do?

    a. Tell the teacher.

    b. Accidentally on purpose spill the tray of bottled paints on those mean kids during art class. Now you can make fun of their color.

    c. Look the other way. You don't want those guys picking on you!

    d. Throw a ball straight at the bullies and then look the other way.

    e. Walk up and tell the boy to ignore those guys and come play with you.

- What might happen if you choose to stick your neck out for this kid?
- Have you ever been called names? How did you feel?
- How do you think God feels about prejudice? (Parents may have to explain this further.)
- Does God love all people the same? How do you know?

3. *(H. Ages 7 and up.)* You have a friend who is very sad because her parents are getting a divorce. She tells you that she plans to run away from home. What would you do?

    a. Pack your bags and plan to run away together to

Alaska on the money you get from suing her parents for child abuse.
   b. Tell her parents how much they are hurting your friend.
   c. Write "Dear Abby" to ask what to do.
   d. Reassure your friend that God loves her and will get her through this hard time.
   e. Tell your friend that you are praying for her and her parents every day.
   • Why is divorce such a difficult thing to go through?
   • When friends are feeling sad, what are some good ways to be a friend to them?
   • Have you ever tried to cheer up a sad friend? What happened?

4. *(H. Ages 11 and up.)* A friend down the street has started acting differently. He goes into the woods with older boys who have gotten into trouble at school for doing drugs. What would you do?
   a. Talk to your parents about it and pray about what to do.
   b. Tell the boy's parents what you have seen and what you know about the other boys.
   c. Sneak into the woods and make howling noises to scare the boys.
   d. Stay inside every day.
   e. Go spy on the boys and take pictures.
   • What is so bad about drugs? Why?
   • What if someone you care about doesn't want your help?
   • What makes a situation like this so difficult?

5. *(M. Ages 11 and up.)* A new family has started coming to your church and the girl is in your Sunday school class. You thought you overheard your parents talking to each other about the girl having AIDS. What would you do?
   a. Tell all your friends so they can stay away from her.
   b. Ask your parents if it is true and talk about the best way to handle it.
   c. Verify the facts, then you and your buddies give the girl the cold shoulder.
   d. Talk to the new girl and try to make her feel welcome. She seems okay.
   e. Wear a purple oxygen mask to Sunday school.

- What happens when someone starts telling rumors?
- AIDS is a terrible disease that some people get through no fault of their own and others get because of sinful behavior. How did Jesus show compassion (love that sees the hurt) to people who were sick?

Keep the Faith

Any length trip. Ages as indicated for each.

"Be joyful in hope, patient in affliction, faithful in prayer." (Romans 12:12)

1. *(M. All ages.)* You've just been told that one of your closest friends is moving to the other side of the country. What would you do?
   a. Throw a going-away party for your friend.
   b. Pack your bags. You're going too!
   c. Cry.
   d. Hide your friend in your closet so he or she can't leave, and slip him or her food after supper.
   e. Make plans for how you are going to keep in touch.

   - What makes some friendships so special?
   - Do your parents have any close friends in faraway places? How do they keep their friendship going?
   - Did Jesus have any special friends? How do you know?

2. *(E. All ages.)* Someone makes fun of you because you go to church with your parents. What would you do?
   a. Ignore it. They don't know what they're talking about.
   b. Make fun of them for something they do that you think is dumb.
   c. Quit going to church.
   d. Take a deep breath and calmly say, "Yes, I go to church because I love God, and I'm not ashamed of it."
   e. Say that you go because you love the snacks or the great food at the potlucks.

   - Why does it hurt so much when people call you names?
   - Do you think Jesus ever got called names? How did He respond?
   - If you are faithful to God, no matter what people say, do you think God will help you when you're hurt or afraid? How do you know?

3. *(E. Ages 7–10.)* You and your family have two flat tires on your way to your first Little League game. What would you do?
   a. Get a sudden surge of adrenaline flowing through you and push the car to the park.
   b. Just wait patiently and be of any help that you can.
   c. Get angry with your parents.
   d. Wave down the first one of your teammate's vehicles you see and beg for a ride.
   e. Use the cell phone to try to call your coach.

   • When unexpected inconveniences occur, it can be irritating. How can your response help or hinder the situation?
   • How does reacting calmly help out?

4. *(E. Ages 7 and up.)* Your Mom told you to practice the piano while she's at the store. You play for three minutes then get distracted by TV. Before you know it, you see your mother pulling into the driveway. What would you do?
   a. Admit what happened and accept the consequences.
   b. Run back to the piano and continue to practice until Mom comes in and tells you that you may stop now.
   c. When your mom asks why you aren't practicing, act dumb, like you didn't understand her directions earlier. Tell her it's the Tower of Babel all over again: God must have confused her language for a time.
   d. Stay put, and hope your mom doesn't ask any questions.
   e. Act like you've got a cramp in your hands from all the practicing.

   • Since you didn't stick with your task this time, how might this affect your mom's trust in you next time she tells you to do something while she's away?
   • Diligence is sticking with something. Why do parents want their children to be diligent with work they need to do?
   • Think of a situation that happened to you today in which you either showed diligence or failed to be diligent. Talk about it.

5. *(E. Ages 7 and up.)* The pastor at your church asked if you would assist him with a demonstration during his sermon this Sunday. You said you would. It's Sunday morning and you have stage fright. What would you do?

a. Call the pastor up before church and say that you're scared and won't be able to do it after all.
b. Wear a large-brimmed hat pulled down low, so that no one can see your face and you can't see them.
c. Moan and groan about feeling bad, hoping you'll be allowed to stay home.
d. Pray to God for help, then grit your teeth and go to church, trusting that God will get you through this somehow.
e. Keep your word and help out, but with a bad attitude. You don't want him asking you again—and with your attitude, you can bet he won't!

- If you do what you say, do others trust you more or less than if you don't?
- Do you like to be given special tasks by your teacher or someone at church? Why or why not?
- How can you build people's confidence in you?

Truthfulness

Any length trip. Ages as indicated for each.

"I have no greater joy than to hear that my children are walking in the truth." (3 John 1:4)

1. *(M. All ages.)* You're out of cash and badly want to buy some trading cards, a special toy, or a candy. There are a few dollar bills lying on top of your brother's dresser. He owes you money, but he is staying at your uncle's house all weekend. What would you do?
   a. Take it but leave a note that says how much you took and when you took it.
   b. Exclaim, "What?" as if hearing a voice from heaven. "There's some money for me on my brother's dresser? Thanks!" Take it and run.
   c. Decide that you won't buy anything today.
   d. Call your brother at your uncle's house and offer to be his slave for life if he'll let you take the money off his dresser.
   e. Ask your mom if you can borrow a few bucks.

   - Was your approach truthful? Why or why not?
   - Will you help or hinder your relationship with your brother by the choice you made?

2. *(E. All ages.)* You and an older friend were throwing a ball in the house and knocked a picture off the wall. The glass broke. Your friend offered to hide the evidence and replace the glass before your mom found out anything. What would you do?
   a. Bring your mom breakfast in bed the next morning to butter her up for the news. Start by listing all the things you did right and all the things you did *not* break.
   b. Let your friend "hide and replace," as suggested.
   c. Clean up the mess and tell Mom when she gets home.
   d. Try to hide the evidence until *after* you have replaced the glass. Then tell Mom.
   e. Blame your friend for everything.
   • Do you like to have friends who aren't truthful? Why or why not?
   • Do you want your mom and dad to tell you the truth when you ask them something? Why or why not?
   • If someone broke something of yours, what would you want him or her to do? Why?

3. *(H. All ages.)* Your parents ask, "What are you thinking about?" You are too embarrassed to tell them. What would you do?
   a. Smile and say, "Oh, nothing that's important."
   b. Launch into an elaborately long but boring story, making them sorry they asked.
   c. Blurt out, "It's none of your business."
   d. Just roll your eyes and sigh.
   e. Tell them, "I'd rather not say."
   • Are some things okay to keep to yourself? How do you know?
   • Are there times that you might not tell *everything* but are still being honest?
   • When could saying exactly what is on your mind hurt someone's feelings? Discuss it.

4. *(E. All ages.)* You have a "friend" at preschool or school who sometimes says mean things to you. What would you do?
   a. Put a "Kick Me—Please!" sticker on his or her back.
   b. Ditch the friend.
   c. Confront the problem. Tell this friend that your feelings get hurt when he or she says those things and you

would like things to change so you can stay friends.
    d. Write mean notes about this person and spread the
        notes around the school.
    e. Talk to your parents about the problem and ask their
        advice.
    •   Do true friends always get along? Why or why not?
        How many sides does friendship have?
    •   What are some ways to confront problems?
    •   How can God help?

5. *(M. Ages 7 and up.)* You didn't study for an important test
    in history that will occur today. You wake up feeling a little
    sick about it. You know that your best friend, who sits next
    to you in class, is a whiz at history. What would you do?
    a. Cram for the test on the way to school and hope for the
        best.
    b. Ask your friend to quiz you on the most important
        points before class.
    c. Determine each answer on the test by playing Eenie,
        Meenie, Minie, Mo.
    d. Put baby powder on your face so you look pale. Act
        dazed and incoherent so you don't have to go to school.
    e. See if you can sneak a peek at your friend's answers
        when the teacher isn't looking.
    •   Why do you think you need to work if you want to
        achieve anything (like studying to make good grades)?
    •   What does God's Word teach about cheating? Why do
        you think it says that?
    •   Do you want people to trust what you do and say? Why
        or why not?

6. *(E. Ages 7 and up.)* It's nearly bedtime and you remember that
    you left your sister's bicycle outside. It's raining and you really
    don't want to get wet. She wouldn't know if it was you or the
    neighbor kid who left it out. What would you do?
    a. Just forget about it. The bike will be there in the morning.
    b. Put on your shoes and raincoat and tell your parents
        you just remembered you have to get your sister's bike
        out of the rain.
    c. Try to convince your dad that he should go get it.
    d. Blame someone else when your sister finds out the
        next day.

e. Claim that you saw the tooth fairy borrowing your sister's bike in the night.

- Is doing what is right always easy? Why or why not?
- How can you decide what is right or wrong?
- How can God's Holy Spirit nudge your conscience? Talk about it.

Forgiving and Restoring Relationships

Any length trip. Ages as indicated for each.

"Bear with each other and forgive whatever grievances you may have against one another. Forgive as the Lord forgave you." (Colossians 3:13)

1. *(M. All ages.)* Your neighbor dropped your favorite beanie in the ditch and it's pretty much soaked with mud. You're not sure if she did it by accident or on purpose. What would you do?
   a. Throw the beanie in the washing machine. Hopefully it will clean up okay.
   b. Take something of your neighbor's and put it where something bad might happen to it, like rolling into the creek or being mangled by a dog.
   c. Confront your neighbor with her irresponsibility. If she apologizes, laugh in her face.
   d. Tell your neighbor what happened and talk about it.
   e. When the neighbor is home alone, sabotage her front door with a bucket of water, and then ring the doorbell and hide.

   - If you decide not to talk to the neighbor, might it happen again?
   - You might make your neighbor angry if you accuse her without proof. What would you say then?
   - How could you approach her in a way that works?

2. *(E. All ages.)* Your brother (or sister) really made you angry this morning. You lost your temper and were very unkind. He (or she) told your parents. Now you're in a heap of trouble and still angry. Your parents are discussing your discipline in the other room. What would you do?

a. Write a contract that states you will never speak to your brother (or sister) again. But if he (she) ever annoys you again, you have every right to say anything you want to him (her), without consequences.
b. Ask God to help you calm down and respond properly to your parents.
c. Sneak out of the window and go to your tree house.
d. Accept your discipline and apologize.
e. Ransack your brother's (or sister's) room. He (or she) is such a pain!

- Why do parents want their children to treat each other nicely?
- How can learning to get along with your brothers and sisters help you get along well in life?
- What do you think God wants? Why?

3. (H. All ages.) Two of your best friends are upset with each other over something really dumb. What would you do?
a. Keep quiet and clear of the situation.
b. Make a big joke out of the whole thing. Maybe if you embarrass everybody enough, they'll see how dumb they're acting.
c. Decide which of your friends you like the best and take his or her side.
d. Try to be a peacemaker by helping your friends understand and forgive each other.
e. Write them each a letter saying they better make up or else. Sign them "Arnold Schwarzenegger."

- What do you think the qualities of a peacemaker are?
- If you don't know, where can you find out?
- What are some difficult aspects of trying to work out a conflict? How can you make them easier?

4. (E. All ages.) Today you told someone a lie and now you have a knot in your stomach and feel like God would probably like to hear from you. You really messed up. What would you do?
a. Run away from God like Jonah did.
b. Just try to forget about what you did. Everyone makes mistakes.
c. Ask God's forgiveness and then ask the person you lied to for forgiveness too.

d. Read your Bible. Maybe it says in there what you should do.

e. Put on sackcloth and ashes, like they did in the Old Testament, and sit in your yard moaning. (It sounds messy, though.)

- Is there anyone who *hasn't* messed up in life?
- How do you know that God wants to have a close relationship with you?
- Where can you find answers when you don't know?

5. *(M. Ages 7 and up.)* Your friend doesn't stick up for you when a bully accuses you of taking his seat on the bus and forces you to move. What would you do?

a. Give your "friend" the cold shoulder. You can find better friends than that!

b. Tell the bus driver that you're being picked on.

c. When you get off the bus, grab a stone and throw it at the departing bus.

d. Call your friend later and talk about what happened. Maybe he or she was too scared to stick up for you.

e. Crawl under the seat of the bus to tie your "friend's" shoelaces to the leg of the seat.

- Why do you think some kids like to bully others?
- How do you think friends should stick up for each other?
- How can you forgive others when they disappoint you?

6. *(M. Ages 7 and up.)* You are hurt and angry with Jimmy because, even though he promised secrecy, he told Susan your most embarrassing moment. You got angry. This is not the first time he has told secrets. What would you do?

a. To get even, tell someone a secret that Jimmy has told you.

b. Tell Jimmy how hurt you feel that he didn't keep the secret. See how he responds.

c. No small mistake is worth losing your friendship with Jimmy. You'll forgive him.

d. Stay angry with Jimmy until *he* comes to *you* to make things right again.

e. Tell Jimmy you received a message from the future warning that if he didn't learn to keep secrets, he'd be abducted by aliens who would replace his ears with mops.

- What are things you want your friends to trust you for?

- Why does making a relationship right again sometimes involve swallowing your own pride? What makes it worth it?
- Why do friends sometimes make mistakes?

Seeking God

Any length trip. Ages as indicated for each.

"Do your best to present yourself to God as one approved, a workman who does not need to be ashamed and who correctly handles the word of truth." (2 Timothy 2:15)

1. *(M. All ages.)* You realize that you have a problem with your temper; you spoke harshly to your sister for giving you bunny ears while your grandma was taking a picture of "her little angels" getting ready for church this morning. You really want to stop reacting so badly when something bothers you. What would you do?
   a. Go back to bed until you're 18 and can move out on your own.
   b. Apologize and pray for help in the future.
   c. Join "Over-Reactors Anonymous."
   d. Tape some helpful Bible verses to the bathroom mirror.
   e. Vow never to have your picture taken with your sister again.

   - Have you ever reacted similarly? What happened?
   - Why are bad tempers so dangerous?
   - Do you think God wants to help people who want to change? Why or why not?

2. *(M. Ages 7 and up.)* You have a tough decision to make about whether to go to summer camp for a week or play soccer in the fall. Unfortunately your parents can't afford to pay for both so you have to choose. What would you do?
   a. Beg your parents. You just *have* to do both! They can work extra to pay for it.
   b. Choose soccer. Then begin bugging your parents so bad that they'll just have to send you to camp as well.
   c. Pray for an idea to earn enough money on your *own* to pay for the second activity.
   d. Toss a coin to make the decision.
   e. Make lists that describe all the good things about each

of the activities and compare them. Base your decision on which of the two activities will be more beneficial to you in the long run.

- How can knowing God's Word help you make decisions, even when the decision isn't a right or wrong issue?
- None of the above options included asking someone for advice. When is that a good idea?
- How do you choose whom to ask for their opinion?

3. *(H. Ages 7 and up.)* You're invited to sit with a friend in church but her little brother keeps pestering you and trying to capture your attention while the service is going on. What would you do?
   a. Play with the little guy.
   b. Move to a different seat.
   c. Kindly ask the little boy to play quietly without you. You want to pay attention to the service.
   d. Give the kid the elbow so his mom has to take him out of the service to calm him down.
   e. Stand up and ask for prayer that the little guy will leave you alone.

   - How would you describe most church services that you have been to?
   - Do you usually go to church wanting to listen to what's being said or sung about? If not, why not?
   - Talk about why Christians go to church. What are some good reasons?

4. *(M. Ages 7 and up.)* Your neighbor friend asks you a question about Jesus or the Bible because she knows that you're a Christian. You don't really know the answer. What would you do?
   a. Fake a response. She won't know the difference.
   b. Tell her that she asked a good question. You'll do some investigating in your Bible and get back to her with the answer.
   c. Tell her you have no idea. Give her your Bible so she can look it up herself.
   d. Tell her that you don't know, so probably no one else does either. She'll just have to live with her ignorance.
   e. Trip and hurt yourself so she'll forget her question. While you're "recovering," look it up in case she asks again.

- Would you know *how* to look up information in the Bible? How?
- Do you feel that you have poor, fair, good, or above average knowledge of the Bible for your age?
- How can you improve your biblical knowledge (besides doing these *Joy Ride!* activities)?

5. *(M. Ages 11 and up.)* Your parents only let you visit certain Internet sites but you can surf anywhere at your friend's place. Your friend logs onto a restricted site that immediately gives you an uneasy feeling. What would you do?
   a. Tell your friend that you don't like that site, please find something else.
   b. Ignore your gut feelings and don't say anything.
   c. Say that your stomach is upset; then throw up on the keyboard so your friend *can't* go to the bad sites.
   d. Wave your hands around and look blank, exclaiming, "Help, help! That Web site just burned my eyes out!"
   e. Challenge your friend about why he or she checks out restricted sites like that when they often have bad content.

   - Why is it risky business to ignore your gut feelings?
   - If you know what God expects, is that a help or hindrance to making good decisions? Why?
   - Are some things always wrong? How do you know?
   - Some people think that there are no absolutes. How can you know the truth?

Humility

Any length trip. Ages as indicated for each.

"Live in harmony with one another. Do not be proud, but be willing to associate with people of low position. Do not be conceited." (Romans 12:16)

1. *(E. All ages.)* You're in a hurry to get your food at the church potluck and go sit with the other kids, but you notice an elderly woman, whom you don't know, having trouble holding her plate while she dishes out her food. What would you do?
   a. Tell the woman to be careful and go on your way.
   b. Tell your friends to save you a spot at the table, put your own plate down, and help the woman by holding

her plate for her.

c. Signal someone standing nearby that this woman needs help.

d. Look away from the woman. You don't want to see what might happen to her plate.

e. Fill four plates at once to show her how much more coordinated you are than she is, and then do cartwheels with them without spilling a drop.

- Did you spot this as an opportunity to be a servant? Why or why not?
- What do you think Jesus would have done? Why?

2. (E. All ages.) You're out of town visiting your grandparents' church. You are in a small Sunday school classroom with 10 other kids. The stomach of the person right beside you starts growling loudly. What would you do?

a. Smile and point to the guilty party.

b. Watch how everyone else reacts and do the same.

c. Just ignore it and hope the other kids don't think it's you.

d. Ask to use the restroom. That way the other kids will hear the stomach growling when you're not in the room.

e. Act as if you're receiving a special message and say, "Come again. I couldn't quite hear that. Reception is unclear."

- Would it make any difference what the stomach growler does? Why or why not?
- How would making a joking comment change the situation?

3. (M. All ages.) You are privileged to have a good group of friends that is admired by your peers. A new boy at preschool or school is having trouble fitting in. The other kids think he looks strange, and he appears to come from a poor family. What would you do?

a. Don't make eye contact with the new boy. You don't want him asking you for any favors.

b. Get up the courage to ask the boy to sit by you at break and get to know him a little.

c. Ask your friends if you can include the new boy in your game at recess.

d. You are too chicken to be seen with the boy at school, but you try to talk with him when you see him at the park on Saturday. Maybe that'll count.

e. Go on a long vacation. Maybe when you come back the new kid will have made other friends, and you will be off the hook.

- Why do kids care so much about what other kids think?
- Do you think grown-ups have the same kinds of trouble? Why or why not?

4. *(E. Ages 7 and up.)* You are a great student. You have had the highest grades in your class all year—until you goofed up one big test in Language and pulled your grade point average down. Now Elizabeth is getting the honors award from the principal instead of you. What would you do?

a. Visit the trophy shop and order a special *big* trophy for *you*.

b. Complain to the teacher about what seems unfair to you.

c. Congratulate Elizabeth and tell her you'll beat her next year.

d. Take out your anger and disappointment on your family when you get home.

e. Realize Elizabeth won fair and square. Even though you're disappointed, tell her she did a good job.

- It is humbling to see someone else get the honor that you were hoping for or expecting for yourself. How well do you handle experiences like this?
- How do others feel when you honor them?
- Is it difficult to honor others above yourself? Why or why not?

5. *(M. Ages 7 and up.)* You knew that your shorts were just a bit too loose. All it took was a grabbing fall from your basketball opponent to pull them down to your knees in front of the whole school. You thought you were going to *die*! What would you do?

a. Turn beet red and dive under the bleachers.

b. Just laugh with everyone else and try to forget about it.

c. Run out of the gym and hide for about a week.

d. Get angry and blame your mother for making you wear loose shorts.

e. Smile, red face and all, and ask the audience, "Anyone have a safety pin?"

- Think of someone you know who handles unexpected situations gracefully. How does he or she do it?
- Is that person able to laugh at him- or herself at times or admit when he or she has made a mistake? How does that help?

6. *(H. Ages 7 and up.)* A new girl at school can sing really well. Until now you've had the best parts in all the musicals. You really want to have the lead role again this time but you aren't sure you will get it. What would you do?
   a. Write a note to the new girl telling her that she better not try out for the part you want.
   b. Try to make friends with the new girl because you feel bad about being jealous. Maybe you can sing a duet.
   c. Look for a good chance to show her up in front of others.
   d. Do your best at the audition and just wait to see what happens.
   e. Come up with a voice demodulator and trick her into swallowing it so her voice sounds awful.

   - Have you ever been the object of jealousy because you were good at something? What was it like? Why is it dangerous to think of yourself too highly?
   - When you compliment *others* for their accomplishments, how do you feel? Why?

Responsibility

Any length trip. Ages as indicated for each.

"Don't let anyone look down on you because you are young, but set an example for the believers in speech, in life, in love, in faith and in purity." (1 Timothy 4:12)

1. *(E. All ages.)* You see a lot of smoke coming out of the window at a neighbor's house. What would you do?
   a. Grab your video recorder and get ready to make the tape of the year. It'll sell to all the news shows and you'll be famous!
   b. Ignore it. They're always burning toast over there.
   c. Call the fire department or 911.
   d. Run over to see what's going on.
   e. Find an adult to do something.

- Would you get in trouble for calling 911 if it didn't end up being an emergency? Why or why not?
- Talk about it. If you didn't act quickly, what might be the result?

2. *(E. All ages.)* You just finished your can of soda at the church carnival. There is a recycling container on the other side of the building but a trash can right in front of you. What would you do?
   a. Use the trash can.
   b. Turn your walk into a game of kick the can. By the time you're done, it'll look like it's been "recycled."
   c. Leave the can on the bench. Maybe someone else will pick it up to recycle it.
   d. Walk around the building to put it in the recycle bin.
   e. Smash the can and stick it in your pocket to deal with later.

   - If you think you should do something, but don't do it, how does it make you feel?
   - Is doing the right thing always convenient? Why or why not?
   - What difference should convenience make?

3. *(H. Ages 7 and up.)* You know you should've received a suspension from school for being disrespectful to the principal but instead she just gave you a warning. She's not even going to call your parents. She told you that she wants *you* to tell them what happened. What would you do?
   a. That was a close one. There's no way you're telling your parents!
   b. Tell your parents half of the truth so they know you went to the principal but they don't blame you for what happened.
   c. Spend the night—two or ten if you have to—at a friend's house.
   d. Talk to your parents like the principal asked you to.
   e. Put on a real show for your parents, telling them every detail, but with overacted emotion and tears so they'll feel sorry for you and not punish you.

   - Will there be consequences if you tell your parents? If you don't?

- Why do you think God has given parents the responsibility to raise their children?
- Why are rules important?

4. *(M. Ages 7 and up.)* Your mom just asked you to vacuum the living room. It's really your sister's turn and you don't feel like doing it. It looks pretty clean already. What would you do?
   a. Vacuum it quickly but not very thoroughly.
   b. Bribe your sister so she'll do it.
   c. Put the vacuum away. It looks good to you.
   d. Go ahead; vacuum it and do an awesome job.
   e. Get a megaphone and hide near your mom. Then, using a deep, important voice, say, "It's (name your sister)'s turn to vacuum. Beware, don't be unfair, or bad things will happen."

   - Which of the choices builds your mother's trust in you?
   - When you do a good job at something, how do you end up feeling about it? Why?

5. *(H. Ages 7 and up.)* You left your backpack at school—again! There is a book report due tomorrow and your book is in the backpack. Your mom told you the last time she made a special trip back to the school that she wasn't going to do it again. What would you do?
   a. Write a crazy but interesting report about a (made-up) book with the same title. Maybe your teacher will give you an A for creativity.
   b. Go to the library. Maybe you'll find the book there or find a friend to study with.
   c. Explain the situation to your mom and see if she'll give in to save your grade.
   d. Get angry with your mom and blame her for the bad grade you're going to get.
   e. Pray about it and get by the best you can. You'll be more responsible with your things from now on.

   - How does avoiding your problems help or not help?
   - Accepting responsibility for your actions is easy. (True or False?)
   - How does a person learn to be more responsible?

6. *(H. Ages 7 and up.)* You promised your little sister that you would play a game with her as soon as you finished your

homework. The phone just rang and you've been invited to play down the street at a friend's house. What would you do?

a. Tell your friend you'll be right down after you finish your homework.

b. Tell your friend that you promised your sister you'd play a game with her. Does he care to join you?

c. Try to make a deal with your sister that you'll play with her even longer later on if she'll let you go now.

d. Play with your sister but act mean to her the whole time.

e. Tell your sister that a powerful magnetic force is pulling you uncontrollably down the street. If you don't go, it'll tear you apart.

• Have you ever experienced someone not doing as they promised? How did you feel?

• How do you want people to respond when you say you will do something? Why?

7. *(M. Ages 11 and up.)* You're not allowed to see PG-13 movies. Your parents gave you permission to go with friends to see a G-rated movie. One of the friend's parents drops you off, but once you're at the theatre your friends head for the PG-13 movie. What would you do?

a. Go to the G movie on your own.

b. Call your parents to come get you.

c. Try to talk your friends out of going to the PG-13 movie. It just isn't right.

d. Go along with them and tell your parents they tied you up and dragged you in there. You had no choice!

e. Pretend to accidentally spill your soda during the first minute of the film. Excuse yourself and sneak over into the G movie.

• Do you think your parents have good reasons for setting boundaries? What might they be?

• Would you feel right about going along with your friends? Why or why not?

• What was difficult about whatever decision you made?

GLOVE COMPARTMENT LESSONS*

These are object lessons using things already in your car or things that you can place in the glove compartment prior to departure. It will help to read over these lessons ahead of time, if possible, to understand what each is about, and to think about how you might introduce the lessons so that they are fun for the kids. You will probably want to spread these out rather than doing one after the other—unless your children are begging for more.

Forget an Appointment?*

Medium. Any length trip. All ages.

Needed: Pocket-sized calendar or other calendar that you use.

Explain that inside the glove compartment is something very important to you. Before you show it to your children tell this little riddle to get them thinking:

> Riddle: *It may not be costly; it may not be gold,*
> *Without it my mind might forget what it's told.*

Next, have them guess what it might be from additional clues you give. You could say things like:

1. This item is very valuable to me, day-to-day, month-to-month.
2. It brings things to my mind that I want to remember.
3. It helps me make wise decisions about what I'm going to do today.
4. It is a record of my past.
5. It helps me know when to say, "No."

You get the picture. You can draw this out as long as you want, depending on your children's enthusiasm and interest. Let them check out the glove compartment and see what you have in there. Discuss their reactions.

- Just like a calendar helps you keep your plans in order, so you need God's help and guidelines to keep your lives in order. How good is your family at keeping plans straight?

- Can you think of a time you goofed by not checking the calendar? What happened?

Rewrite*

Easy. Any length trip. Ages 7 and up.

Needed: Pen and piece of paper for each child.

Give each child a pen from the glove compartment and a piece of paper. Challenge them to write down a list of things that they wish they could have done differently or not at all that day. Give a time limit, if you like. When they're done, have them look over the list and pick out an item they wish they hadn't done or that they weren't happy about. Then tell them that all they have to do is erase that item and it simply won't have occurred. In fact, you will give a reward to whoever is the first to erase (without tearing the paper or scribbling over the words) the unwanted item on the list. How? Well, the pen has an eraser, doesn't it? Oh, it doesn't. That is a problem. What to do? Guess no one will have late night privileges this time. Sorry.

- The point is that the ink pen is like your actions. Once you do them, you can't erase them. You might be able to ask forgiveness or do something to fix a situation, but you won't be able to go back in time and change what you did.
- When you think of it this way, how important do you think your decisions are?

Rain's a Comin'*

Easy. Any length trip. All ages.

Needed: An umbrella.

Have a child in the back seat carefully open an umbrella and hold it over his or her head. Let the child hold it there for a while and enjoy seeing the reaction of people in other cars. Have the children count the number of smiles they create. Reward them with a nickel for each smile or something like that. Ask your children if they feel more protected than before they had the umbrella. No? If it was raining (and maybe it is) and they had to get out of the car, would they feel more protected with the umbrella or without it? Why?

- Now think about standing under the umbrella of God. If you make decisions based on God's wisdom, can you think of bad consequences that you will avoid?
- What kind of protection does God provide?

Clueless*

Moderate. Any length trip. All ages.

Needed: A can of food with the label torn off that your kids would like.

Place the can in your glove compartment prior to departure. Tell your children that there is something new in the glove compartment to help them think about a value you want them to learn more about.

Riddle: *It rhymes with man, but it's not a fan.*
It's closed up tight, not budging a mite.

After going through the alphabet trying to think of a rhyming word, surely someone will think of *can*. Get out the can and let your children hold it. Now make a game out of trying to guess what is in it. Count how many guesses it takes to get it right. If the solution is difficult, give a clue now and then. Whoever finally guesses correctly is given the can as a reward.

- How useful is a closed can if there's no label to tell you what is inside?
- Would you buy a can if you didn't know what it was? Why or why not?
- Does God want you to be like a closed, unlabeled can, or an open can where people can see what's inside? Why?
- What good stuff is inside you that God wants others to know about?

Don't Bite!*

Easy. Trips longer than 15 minutes. All ages.

Needed: A lollipop for each child.

Pull a lollipop out of the glove compartment for each of your children. Tell them that today you are having a contest to see who can lick away their lollipop the quickest. Only licking and sucking on the lollipop are allowed. No biting! Go. (If you just have one child, perhaps you can join in the contest—or simply time how quickly he or she can lick the lollipop away.) Declare the winner at the end of the licking race.

Now let's talk about the lollipop. What was it like?

- How is love like a lollipop? Here are some ideas to get you going. It's very sweet, and you enjoy those whom you love. It's sticky, and sometimes love gets a little sticky because you have conflicts and problems with people you love. The temptation to bite the lollipop is like the way you feel sometimes when you are tempted to look out only for yourself and say or do something mean. You need to continue loving patiently and forget about biting that lollipop.

Spread It Around*

Moderate. Trips longer than 30 minutes. All ages.

Needed: A bottle of body lotion of some kind.

Get out a bottle of lotion and hand it to the kids. Have them read the ingredients on the bottle as best they can. Then ask them, "Now, what's lotion supposed to do?" They will give a variety of answers. "Okay now, you're holding the lotion. Do your hands feel softer or smoother?" They'll laugh and think you are silly for being so ridiculous. Of course you have to squeeze the lotion *out* of the bottle to get any benefit. It doesn't do anyone any good stuck in the bottle.

If you dare, allow the children to carefully squeeze all of the lotion out of the bottle into a large zip-lock bag. Zip it shut, gently pushing most of the air out. For safety's sake, stick that bag into another one and zip the second one shut, also pushing out excess air. The kids will be begging to hold the bag. Just let them enjoy feeling the gooey lotion by rolling the bag around on their hands and laps.

Tell them, "Okay. *Now* your hands are smooth and soft because you took the lotion out of the bottle." More sighs of disbelief! How could Mom or Dad be so dense? "Then how is this lotion ever going to give you soft and smooth hands?"

- How is love like that? Love doesn't do any good if it's kept inside, all bottled up. You have to share it—spread it around. Love can smooth over many rough places and make things right between people. Try it with a brother, sister, or friend today.

How Do You See It?*

Moderate. Any length trip. All ages.

Needed: Straws for everyone and a small, clear jar with a lid that will fit into your glove compartment. Fill the jar halfway with a delicious fruit juice and screw on the lid tightly.

Riddle: *Some will see one thing, and some see another.*
Throw a lit match inside and you'll put out the fire.

Let children try to guess what the object is. (Get out the jar and let the children hold it.) What do they see? Some people see a jar half full while others see a jar half empty. How about them? How can this jar of liquid help them remember how God wants them to look at life?

- Discuss the ideas that are given, then add the following: As Christians, faith is believing what you do not see and trusting God for what's ahead. If you look at life with hope and trust in God, it's like looking at a jar that is half full, and trusting God to continue to fill it.
- Pass out the straws and let the kids drink up the juice.

Patience Is a Virtue*

Easy. Trips longer than 20 minutes. All ages.

Needed: Three or four rolls of pennies for each child.

When you get in the car, have each child hold his or her hands in a cup shape. Then reach into your glove compartment and pull out the coins. Start pouring all the coins into the children's hands, filling them as full as possible. Tell them that if they can hold on to their coins without dropping them—and without a *word* of complaint for the duration of the drive—they will be allowed to keep the coins! (Try to help out by driving smoothly.)

While driving, you may notice some fidgeting or discomfort after a while. Try to ignore it. You want them to fight through any discomfort to reach the goal you gave them.

If a child is able to make it through the trip without complaining or dropping any coins, follow through with your reward: They can keep the coins. You may wish to give some of the coins as a reward if a few coins slid off accidentally but there was no complaining involved. If a child just can't help but utter, "This is getting tiring," or, "When is it going to be over?" then just let them complain, but at the end of the trip take away all of their coins with a pleasant comment that you hope they had fun trying—but it's too bad they didn't make it without complaining. Since they complained, you get your coins back.

- Talk about how difficult or not difficult it was for them to keep their comments to themselves. For some kids this will not have been hard at all. For others, sitting with hands in one position for 20 minutes will have seemed like an eternity.
- Stress that God wants them to learn patience. Much of life will require it. Children can learn patience in small ways each day.
- Congratulate those who did well with their attitude. Tell your children that you will be watching to see other ways that they display patience in the coming days.

Coming Attractions*

Moderate. Trips longer than 30 minutes. All ages.

Needed: Colorful brochure about a tourist attraction that your children have not been to but would enjoy seeing if they had the chance.

Tell the children that you have something for them to look at. Hand them the brochure. Tell them that you want them to look it over carefully and tell you all about what is said and shown at this attraction. (Younger children can concentrate on the pictures.)

As you drive, let the children tell you all about it. Ask any questions you want. When they're done, ask them if they think you should trust what the brochure says. In other words, just because the brochure says there is a (giant slide or whatever), can you really believe that it is true? Pose several questions in this way and see how determined the children are to convince you that it *is* true.

- Just like you trust what the brochure tells you about a certain attraction having this or that, you have to trust God that what He says is true.

- What is God's brochure that tells you what you can expect from Him? (The Bible.)
- Encourage your children, whenever they have trouble trusting God for something, to read more in God's brochure—it will help them learn about trusting and being faithful to God.

It All Adds Up*

Hard. Trips longer than 30 minutes. Ages 7 and up.

Needed: Calculator and store receipt listing several items.

Tell the children that the item they are going to find in the glove compartment will help you prove that the store is cheating you. It shows that the store does not tell you the correct amount you owe when you go there. Get the calculator out of the glove compartment and hand it and the receipt to the children. Tell them that you want them to add up everything on the list to see what they come up with. While they are adding, make a comment that you think one of the items on the list should be a much lower price, so please use the new number that you give them. For instance, you might say, "By the way, they charged more than I wanted to pay for that shampoo, so just add in $1.50 instead of $2.50 for it."

This should lead into a whole debate. The kids will insist that you can't *choose* how much you want to pay at the store. The store tells you how much it is and you either choose to buy it or not. If you don't think you paid the correct price, you would have to go back to the store and check on it. But you can't just make up your own prices.
- Let the children finish their adding and give you their verdict on whether or not the store has added correctly.
- Talk about how to know whether something is true or not. Can you test it? In this case, if the price is truly in question, you would have to go back to the store. In other situations in life, getting at the truth means knowing and understanding the source.
- Where do you go to test the truth? Discuss how the Bible is that source.

Mirror, Mirror on the Wall*

Easy. Any length trip. All ages.

Needed: A mirror.

Take a mirror out of your glove compartment. Give it to your children and ask them to look in the mirror and imagine what the mirror would picture if it could show them anything they wanted. Maybe their brother would turn into a green tree frog. Maybe your car would look like a Porsche, etc. Allow everyone to get a little silly.

Finally, ask questions about the things the children actually see and whether they like what they see or not. Ask them why the mirror can't give a different picture than what is truly there. For instance, if your child sees an icky piece of candy stuck to the seat, ask why the mirror can't make the candy look brand new and the seat look like a new Porsche seat?

- The point is, just as a mirror reflects exactly what is real, your life reflects what is really inside you. If people choose to try to lie or cover up the truth, eventually the truth will come out.
- Jesus said that a good tree bears good fruit and a bad tree bears bad fruit. Trees are known by their fruit. Talk about what this means.

Weekend Silly Drive*

Moderate. A special hour or more drive. Ages 7 and up.

Needed: A local roadmap, highlighted to show the route you need to take to get where you are going. Consider going somewhere the kids aren't familiar with on a route that has a number of turns. Allow a few "orientation" minutes in the car before you begin your ride.

Today the children have the privilege of being your navigator(s). Retrieve the prepared map from the glove compartment and hand it to the kids. Show them on the map exactly where you are and where you need to go, following the highlighted route. Also show them precisely where the names of the roads are located and how to determine whether to turn right or left when looking at the map.

Unless your children have had previous experience reading maps, it might be too difficult for them to give you accurate directions by looking at the map. Help them by asking specific questions like, "Okay, we are on _____ Road. What is the name of the road we need to turn on next?" Make sure they feel like they've done their job. If they give wrong directions, go along with them.

Make this drive as confusing as possible by purposely messing up—especially if your children give excellent instructions. Say things like, "I think I know a shortcut" and turn on a different street. Or, "No, that can't be right—this way feels right" and turn down another road. Finally, pull over somewhere and try to tell your children it's their fault that you are lost. After an animated discussion, continue to your destination.

- Talk about what happened when you got off course.
- Why did it matter if you stayed on the right streets?
- The highlighted map is like following the truth or living in truth. What happens if you stray from the path of truth that God has laid out for your lives?
- The Bible says that God's way is not the straightest and easiest way. It is sometimes narrow and windy. How can you keep checking to make sure you stay on the right path?

A Little First Aid*

Easy. Any length trip. All ages.

Needed: Bandages—lots of them!

Ask, "What come in a box and are sticky almost all over?"

Second clue, if needed: "They come in different shapes and stick to elbows and knees."

Once your children get it, get out the bandages and let them go wild with them (just this once!). You will judge the silliest looking bandage job. Have fun.

- Ask why bandages are used.
- What are the characteristics of a bandage?
- What keeps the bandage from falling off? Can you think of ways to "bandage" hurt relationships to promote healing?
- Does this ever get a little sticky? (You bet! It's often not easy, but it's worth the effort.)

Airplane Challenge*

Easy. Any length trip. All ages.

Needed: Container of tissues.

Grab the tissues. It's time for a good cry! Just kidding. Challenge the kids to a paper airplane contest. Hand out the tissues for them to do their folding magic. (Now, unless you have unusually stiff tissues, the kids are going to have a little problem with this challenge.) Talk about the tissue. If it's no good for making paper airplanes, what good is it? (Wiping runny noses, etc.) What type of tissue do they prefer to blow their noses with—a soft kind or a stiff kind? Why?

- What would be an example of a "messy" situation between people that needs "cleaning up?"
- What kind of "tissue" would be most helpful in cleaning up the matter—a soft, gentle type or a rough, stiff type?
- Describe actions in terms of being soft and gentle or rough and stiff (for example, an apology is soft, blaming is hard or rough).
- How do you like people cleaning up messes with you (soft or hard)? Why?

Plug Your Nose!*

Easy. Any length trip. All ages.

Needed: A parent who smells good or not so good! (Before this activity, consider how you could smell either really bad or really good for this discussion. For instance, use an opportunity when your clothes smell of smoke because you've been at a smoker's house, you are obviously perfumed, or you're wearing your yummy smelling fresh-cookies-from-the-oven sweater or blouse.)

Okay, everyone is climbing in and remarking about the smell. If they politely don't comment, ask what they smell or if they notice anything. Ask questions like:

- Do I have a good or bad aroma?
- What do you think makes me smell this way today?
- How does the aroma tell you what I've been up to?
- How does it affect your desire to be around me?
- Have everyone name their top three favorite smells and their three least favorite smells.

- There are "spiritual" or "emotional" aromas too. What might they be? Name some good and bad ones.
- Second Corinthians 2:14–15 says, "Through us spreads everywhere the fragrance of the knowledge of him. For we are to God the aroma of Christ among those who are being saved and those who are perishing." Talk about ways to be the aroma of Christ. Why is it important? Name a few people you know who have Christ's aroma.
- What aroma do you give off? Are people getting a pleasing "whiff" from you?

Prayer Snacks*

Easy. Any length trip. All ages.

Needed: A tasty snack.

When your kids are commenting about their hunger or when you sense they could use a little pick-me-up, bring out some snacks as a surprise. As they're happily chowing down, talk about how snacks are beneficial. (They help satisfy hunger; they give energy; if they're healthy snacks they add nutrition to your diet without taking the place of a complete meal; they're quick and convenient.)

- Just as snacks can benefit your bodies, so prayer time with God benefits your spirits. How can you have short little prayer snacks with God each day? (You know, short conversations thanking God for the little things or requesting wisdom.)
- God wants to have these little "snacks" of prayer with you each day. The short prayers don't take the place of a longer, more in-depth prayer time, but little talks with God (anytime, anywhere) can provide renewed energy and awareness of God's presence.

Footloose*

*Easy. Any length **night** drive. All ages.*

Needed: Flashlight with working batteries.

In your dark vehicle, ask each child to describe what he or she thinks every person in the car has on his or her feet. People are not to say anything about their own feet until each person has guessed. (And no peeking!)

Now get the flashlight out and let the kids look to see if they were right about which shoes/socks/stockings people are wearing. Warn them to be careful to point the light downward so they don't interfere with the driver's mirror or sight.

Parents are usually pretty good at making sure their kids wear appropriate footwear. For example, they suggest wearing sneakers rather than sandals for a hike in the woods.

- Think of the *worst* shoes to wear to the following destinations: the beach (how about high heels?); on a mountain hike; to the moon; to a wedding; to a funeral; shopping at the mall; to a winter ski competition; to the desert.
- Psalm 119:105: "Your word is a lamp to my feet and a light for my path." Are your "feet" equipped for your spiritual journey?
- Ask God to provide you with just the right "shoes" for each situation you face in life. Through sad times, God can provide the shoes of "strength," and so on.
- What other kinds of shoes does God provide? (For happy times, sick times, temptation times, fearful times . . .)

Calling for Help*

Easy. Any length trip. All ages.

Needed: Cellular or digital phone.

Riddle: *What do you call a pay phone in jail?*
Answer: *A cell phone.*

Tell stories about a time you needed to call for help. Let everyone who wants to share a story do so.

What would you do *today* if you got stranded in your car? Who would you call? Hand the children the cell phone and see if they actually know the number (without completing the call). In fact, if your children don't know how to operate the cell phone, it is wise to teach them so that they know what to do in an emergency.

- What might happen if you were too proud to ask for help?
- Everybody needs help sometimes. It's okay to admit it. Talk about reasons that cause people to be stubborn and not admit they need assistance.

20/20 Vision*

Easy. Any length trip. All ages.

Needed: Sunglasses.

Get the sunglasses out of the glove compartment and let the kids put them on. Ask them if the glasses change anything about their perspective? How and why?

Three-D glasses help you see a movie in 3-D. Decoder glasses help you read something no one else can see. Imagine putting on a pair of glasses that can do something outrageous. What would they want their special glasses to help them see? For example, see into the past to watch the dinosaurs, show them buried treasure, or magnify things so large they can see into space better than an observatory telescope!

- What would you do? (Have fun coming up with ideas.)
- Now imagine a special pair of glasses that could help you see needs around you better so that you could see ways to serve others. Would a pair of those glasses be useful? Why or why not?
- How easy is it to overlook needs that are right around you? Try wearing these imaginary glasses often.

Say Cheese*

Easy. Trips longer than 30 minutes. All ages.

Needed: Camera loaded with film. A disposable camera would work great, too.

Take the camera out of the glove compartment and tell the children they may take turns taking pictures with the camera of whatever they wish until the film is finished.

When the children are done, talk about the pictures taken. Did anyone try to get in the way of someone else's picture? (Why is that so fun for kids?) What pictures will your children wish to keep as a photo memory? Were any pictures taken that someone in the car hopes won't turn out when the film gets developed?

- Try to think of your life as a series of snapshots. What memories of you do you want to leave in other people's minds? What does God see?
- How can you live your life so that you will leave good "pictures" for memories?

Bad Hair Day*

Easy. Any length trip. All ages.

Needed: Hairbrush or comb.

Have a little fun talking about hairdos and bad hair days. Have everyone tell about their worst hair day—or the weirdest hairdo they've ever had! (Be honest, Mom and Dad. Remember your crazy youth?)

Pull the hairbrush or comb out of the glove compartment. Ask why they use a brush or comb on their hair. What does it do? (Gets the tangles out, disciplines the hair . . .) Does a brush or comb ever hurt to use? (Yes, if there are lots of tangles.)

- What are some ways you discipline yourself? (Exercise, eating good foods, study habits, reading the Bible, praying, trying your best to obey, . . .)
- When can discipline be painful?
- Can other people look at your life and tell if you are disciplined or not? Why?
- What areas of discipline do you want to work harder at? How can you do that?

FROM HERE TO THERE

The following items can help you engage your children in meaningful conversations related to particular destinations.

A wacky opening question gets the fun going and additional questions help spark teachable moments.

Going Clothes Shopping

Easy. Any length trip. Ages 7 and up.

What if dressing like a clown—makeup and all—was the fad?
- How would you dress?
- Where would you shop?
- What are your goals for shopping today?

- What is the silliest thing that you have ever worn (to be in style or not)?
- How much can you spend and what are your purchase priorities?
- Can you be in style and still be you? Can you still be modest?
- How can you dress with style and stay on a budget?
- What are the most important things to consider when looking at clothes today?
- Are your priorities different from, say, a child in the country of Kenya? Why or why not?
- How can you take this same $20 (or whatever) and make it stretch the farthest?
- Do you want to do that? Why or why not?

Going to a Kids' Restaurant
Easy. Any length trip. All ages.

Imagine that the restaurant today breaks out into a huge food fight.

- What would that be like?
- How do you imagine it would end?
- See if you can think of three silly slogans that you can say about this restaurant. (For example, "The Best Grease in Town!" "Talk's Cheap, and So's Our Food.")
- How does this restaurant advertise to kids?
- Do you like the way they advertise? Why or why not?
- Are there often movie or toy promotions (in kids' meals) at the restaurant? If so, what kinds of values are being promoted through the toys or movies?
- How can you judge if something is good or bad?

Going to a Concert
Moderate. Any length trip. Ages 7 and up.

Using actual people (ones you know personally or famous people), formulate your very own "Ultimate Disaster Band." In other words, name people to your "Ultimate" band who have absolutely the worst musical talent that you can think of! Perhaps your Uncle George can't carry a note. Or your best friend Rachel *always* sings off key. You can name people to play instruments who have no talent or ability in that area.

- How long do you think you could stand to listen to your "disaster" of a band?
- Can you think of anyone who would want to listen to them?
- What are you hoping to hear at this concert you're going to today?
- What is it that you like most about the artist or group you're going to hear?
- What do you know about the personal lives of the artists?
- How important are the words to the songs that you listen to?
- What are some ways to evaluate what you listen to, to make sure it is good?

Going to a Movie
Moderate. Any length trip. All ages.

If you were hired to direct a movie about a day at your house, what events or elements should be included to make it a hilarious comedy?
- Remember to talk about your family's silliest moments.
- Discover the silliest moments Mom and Dad can remember from their childhoods.
- What are you hoping to experience today as you go see this movie?
- Do you feel you chose it carefully?
- Is this a movie that you think God would approve of? Why or why not?
- If this movie turns out to be different than you expect, what should you do?

On the Way Home from the Movie
Moderate. Any length trip. All ages.

- How many kernels of popcorn do you think you ate?
- How many M&Ms were in the bag?
- On a scale of 1 to 10 (10 being great), how do you rate the movie you just saw?
- Would you recommend it to a friend? Why or why not?
- Did any parts make you feel uncomfortable? Why?
- What values were being promoted?

- Do you think Jesus would have enjoyed watching this movie?
- What would you have done differently if you were the writer or director?

Going to a Church Social Activity

Easy. Any length trip. All ages.

Try for a moment to imagine a potluck that is really "the bomb"—that is, the absolute *best* potluck this side of heaven. Name all of your favorite foods that would be at the potluck.

- Would everyone have a good time eating all your favorite foods? Why or why not?
- How do you feel about attending church events in general?
- What are some reasons that Mom and Dad like to go to church events?
- What can you do for others at this event?
- How is your church like or not like a family? Does it feel like a family to you? Why or why not?
- What are elements of a good family?
- What is the funniest thing you can remember happening at a church gathering?

Going to a Birthday Party

Easy. Any length trip. All ages.

If you had $1,000 to plan a totally wacky surprise party for your best friend, where would you hold the party, and what would it be like?

- Who would you invite (Ronald McDonald? Goofy? . . .)
- How would your friend react?
- What happened at the last birthday party you attended?
- What do you expect today? Who do you expect to see?
- Is there anything that makes you uncomfortable at parties?
- How can you show thankfulness to your friend and his or her parents for inviting you to this party?
- What things do your friends do that make you feel the happiest?
- What kinds of things happen between good friends?
- What could you do today to help this be a very special party for your friend?

Going to the Grocery Store

Easy. Short trips. All ages.

Imagine that you were shopping at the grocery store and all of a sudden the lights were turned out and the announcer told everyone that it was the store's 10th anniversary. To celebrate, for the next three minutes shoppers could participate in a "blind grocery race." You can get all the groceries you can find and carry in the dark—free!

- What would you try to find first?
- How much of what kind of food would you try to find and hold onto in the dark?
- How much fun would that be?
- What might Jesus' favorite food have been? His mother probably loved to make it for Him!
- What foods do you suppose people in the Bible bought from a market?
- How do you think you can search for the best value in what you are buying today?
- Do you think your family has good nutritional habits? Why or why not?
- What are ways you could take better care of your body?
- Sharing food with others is a wonderful way to show love and hospitality. What could you buy or make and share with someone today?

Going to Church

Easy. Any length trip. All ages.

Have a contest to see who can remember the most songs sung last Sunday at church. Or see who can name the most church songs or hymns, period. Give points to each person who calls out a song. Then decide what you would do in church today if you were in charge (take everyone to the park for an outreach?).

- What are your favorite songs at church?
- Do you feel that your mind is prepared to go to church today? Why or why not?
- If you could change something about your worship service, what would it be? Why?
- Why is going to church important?

- What do you talk about in Sunday school?
- Do you enjoy being with your friends at church? Why?
- What do you gain from going to church?

Going to an Amusement Park

Easy. Any length trip. All ages.

If there were an amusement park the size of your whole state or province, what new kinds of rides would you put in it?

The thing you're looking forward to most today is _____.

- What things will determine if you have a blast today?
- What is your plan to be patient and kind to each other today?
- How much money do you need to spend today in order to have fun?
- If you have only two dollars to spend for the whole day, what will you spend it on?

Going to Your Grandparents' House

Easy. Any length trip. All ages.

Imagine that something zapped your grandparents so that they were suddenly your age. What would they be like? What would you enjoy doing with them? What kinds of mischief do you think they would lead you into?

- Why do you think your grandparents love you so much?
- What do you love about them the most?
- What's the funniest story one of your grandparents ever told you?
- What traits have your grandparents passed on to their children [your parents]?

Going to the Dentist (or Doctor)

Moderate. Any length trip. All ages.

Just for fun, imagine a dentist's (or doctor's) worst nightmare! For instance, looking into the mouth of people who have never brushed their teeth in their lifetime, or waking up in a cold sweat from a dream that he/she was being invaded by an army of marching molars armed with toothpicks. Come up with a handful of hilarious scenarios that might occur in a dentist's (or doctor's) dreams.

- How do you feel about going to the dentist (or doctor) today? Are you excited? (Not!)
- What happened last time?
- If you have any cavities (or illnesses), do you think you should be told about them? Why or why not?
- Can you ignore something like a cavity and have it go away?
- Why is it important to know the truth?

Going to Preschool or School

Easy. Any length trip. All ages.

If money were no object, what would be the coolest kind of preschool or school you could think of? (Classrooms on a spaceship, school on a cruise ship with awesome food, . . .)

If you could change one thing about your school day, what would it be?

- What parts of school are your favorites? What parts are your least favorites?
- Is there anything in the way other children treat you that makes you unhappy?
- What would other children say about the way you treat them?
- When something frustrates you at school, what do you do?
- How do you feel about your school?
- Do other children know that you go to church—or that you're a Christian?
- How do you feel about that?
- Why is it important to study and do your best in school?

Going Home from Preschool or School

Easy. Any length trip. All ages.

What is the funniest thing that happened today at preschool or school?

- If you had the chance to make any school announcement

you wanted over the intercom, what would you say? ("School's cancelled for today"?)
- What is the most interesting thing you did today at preschool or school?
- Was anything taught that you disagreed with?
- Do your teacher's lessons agree with the Bible?
- What happened today that made you feel happy?
- Is there anything that happened today that upset you?
- What do you want to do to relax when you get home?
- What would be the ultimate after-school snack?

Going to a Playground

Easy. Any length trip. All ages.

What would the ultimate playground have? Be crazy—monkey bars towering six stories above a pile of hay, free ice cream in giant cones, . . . !
- What kinds of races or contests can you have just for fun at the playground today?
- If someone pushes you or cuts in front of you, what would a wise response be?
- If you are tempted to say something unkind, what should you do instead?
- What do you like most about going to the playground?

Going on Vacation

Easy. Long trips. All ages.

Invent some of the wildest, most ridiculous, out-of-this-world vacations that you can think of. (For example, take a space shuttle to Venus for a really great tan; stay at Snow White's castle and be pampered by the seven dwarves; stay in Tarzan's tree house.)
- What are the *best* parts of going on vacation?
- What was the greatest vacation you've ever had? Why?
- What was the worst? Why?
- How can your family grow together when you're on vacation?
- How do you irritate each other?
- If you could choose anywhere in the world to go on a vacation (for real), where would it be?
- Who would you take with you?

Going Somewhere on a Sunny Day

Moderate. Any length trip. All ages.

On a sunny day, you need to have your sunscreen handy, right? What other "screens" do you wish someone would invent to protect you? (For example, bully screen, lecture screen, fat screen.) What kind of bottle would it come in and how would you apply it? (Be totally silly; e.g., the "bully screen" comes in an aerosol bottle. Just spray the person who is starting to bully you, and he or she mutters compliments out of control for five minutes. Or the "TV screen" looks a lot like wire cutters and prevents the TV from working.)

- What does a sunny day do for your attitude?
- What kind of feeling is it to be "warm" all over?
- What are ways that you can be sunshine on someone else's day?
- Is it more fun to be around someone who is happy or sad? Why?
- When you feel sad, what are things you can do to feel happier?
- Do you like to help other people feel happy? Why or why not?
- Do you think Jesus made people happy or sad? Why?

Going Somewhere in a Storm

Easy. Any length trip. All ages.

If you could make a magical storm that would rain down whatever you wish, what would you wish for? (Showers of candy? A snowfall in the middle of summer?)

- What is the biggest storm you can remember being in?
- How do you feel about storms? Some people love them. Why do you think they do?
- Where do you feel the safest?
- What are things you can do if you get scared?
- There are other "storms" in life that you will face. What are some similarities in how you respond to a thunderstorm and how you can respond to these other stormy times?

Going Someplace You've Never Been Before

Moderate. Any length trip. All ages.

Have each person guess two things they have no way of knowing that you might find at this new place (e.g., there is a blue fence and they sell sodas for $1). See who gets at least one of his or her guesses right.

- What do you expect to experience at this new place?
- Where did you get the information that gives you your impressions about this place?
- Can you trust your source? Why or why not?
- What will you do if you get there and it's not what you expect?
- God gives you information on how life works, like the information you had about this place. Which is easier (or smarter)—to trust God's information and do it His way or to guess what will work? Why?

Going to a Ballgame

Easy. Any length trip. All ages.

If you could play ball with all the talent of any player for one day, who would it be? What would it be like to be a superstar athlete? (All the free athlete's foot spray you wanted.) Take turns having fun with this.

- Do you have any sports heroes? Who are they and why are they your heroes?
- If you were a superstar athlete and were going to do a television commercial to promote a product, what would you want to promote? What would be your catchy slogan? (Take turns thinking of silly slogans.)
- Would you like to be somebody's hero? In what way?
- What are you looking forward to the most at this ballgame?
- What does being a good sport mean to you?

Going to a Friend's House

Easy. Any length trip. All ages.

If you could give your friend the ultimate house, what would it have in it? (A swimming pool full of Jello? A two-story slide into the pool?)

Imagine that you and your friend could star in your very own after-school television series. What setting would you like the show to take place in (Mars, Disneyland, the basement)? Who would play the other characters on the show? What funny scenes would you "replay" from your real life adventures? What would you want other kids to learn from your television show?

- What is the thing you like the most about this friend?
- What do you think he or she likes the most about you?
- What are you looking forward to doing at your friend's house today?
- What are ways that you can show respect and honor to your friend's parents?

Going to a Nice Restaurant

Moderate. Any length trip. All ages.

Can you think of some goofy new restaurant names that would sound like unique places to eat? Some examples might be The Food Fight Café, The Greasy Spoon Drive Thru, Make Your Own Pizza Parlor, Skate While You Eat Diner.

- Do you like to go places where you are expected to act "grown up"? Why or why not?
- When do you think a baby becomes a child? What changes?
- When do you think a child becomes an adult? Why?
- What do you need to learn before you are grown up and on your own?
- What are adults hoping for when they go to a nice restaurant?
- What are some ways you can patiently wait while your food is being prepared?

Going on a Hike

Moderate. Any length trip. All ages.

Have a little fun naming five to 10 things that come to mind in completing the statement,

"You know you're in bad shape when you consider it a major hike to _____." (Examples: get the mail, go to bed, answer the doorbell, . . .)

What would the five grandest hikes imaginable be, even if they are not possible? (Examples: hike up the side of a pyramid, hike the highest underwater mountain, . . .)

- Exercise helps keep your body running properly. Why do you think God made people that way?
- How important is it to take care of your body?
- Do you think God made everything with or without a plan? Why do you think so?
- What does nature tell you about God?
- Why do you think many of the Psalms use descriptions of streams, green grass, mountains, valleys, and so on?
- How many different houses can you find today that God made for His creatures?

Going to a Team Practice

Easy. Any length trip. Ages 7 and up.

Make up a silly team sport. (Blindfold Volleyball, Backwards Baseball, Cow Stacking, Velcro Ball, . . .) What would the rules be? How would you practice?

- Why do you need to practice when you belong to a team? What good does it do?
- Does practice consist of going over things you can already do? Why or why not?
- What about learning new things? Or both?
- What good is physical/mental discipline?
- What makes a good coach?
- Why are good leaders important?
- What would you have your team doing at practice if you were the coach?

BUMPER STICKER FUN

Here are some slogans that you might encounter on car bumpers on any drive. Read the slogan, and then use the questions that accompany it to lead into discussions that help you pass on your values. Look for other bumper stickers to use in a similar way. Alternatively, have fun making up slogans, then talking about what they would mean, and the effect they would have on people.

"The way I drive I've *got* to have faith."

Easy. Any length trip. Ages 7 and up.

- What would you think about the driver of this vehicle?
- Is this sticker intended to be funny or serious—or both?
- What are characteristics of a wise driver?

"Respect ALL life WOMB to TOMB."

Hard. Any length trip. All ages.

In a three-minute time slot have players name as many different characteristics of or adjectives for the way people look as they can. (Short, skinny, blond, freckled, . . .) (Although younger children might have trouble with the slogan, they can certainly help with this part.) Try to keep track of how many are named. Go!

- Why do you suppose God made everyone, all life, different?
- What comes to your mind when you think about this bumper sticker phrase?
- Who is the giver of life?
- How has God displayed His love for us? When did God's love for you begin?

- What should your attitude be toward all people? Why?
- How did God make people different from animals?

Make up some similar lighthearted sayings:

"Respect all life, from the _____ to the _____." (e.g., from the farmhouse to the White House, or from the ice cream parlor to the pizza place).

(*For children ages 11 and up*: You may wish to talk about the deeper issues this brings to mind such as abortion or euthanasia. What is your stand on them? Why?)

"If you don't like the way I drive, get off the sidewalk."

Moderate. Any length trip. All ages.

- What is this driver admitting to?
- What do you think his or her attitude in other areas of life might be? Why?

Fill in the blanks to match other slogans:

If you don't like the way I _____, get off the _____.
(e.g., If you don't like the way I sit, get off the counter.)

"Honk if you love Jesus."

Easy. Any length trip. All ages.

- Would you honk? Why or why not?
- Why might some Christians who love Jesus choose not to honk?
- What could happen if you forgot you had this sticker on your car and people started honking at you?

Have some fun coming up with similar, funny bumper stickers:

_____ if you love _____. (e.g., Smile if you love your dentist.)

"I'd rather be fishing."

Easy. Any length trip. All ages.

What would *you* rather be doing? (Be silly as well as wishful.)
Make up your own bumper sticker.

What would some other people's bumper stickers say that would be humorous? "I'd rather be _____." (Shopping/the president/driving a better car . . .)

- Why can't you always do what you would really like to do?
- Does this bumper sticker sound like a complaint or a fun-loving wish?
- When does telling the truth about how you feel become a complaint? (Parents love to hear their children complain—it sounds so good to the ears. *Not*!)

"CROSS Training."

Moderate. Any length trip. Ages 7 and up.

- What does cross training mean in athletics? If you could be cross trained in any number of areas that you desire, not just athletics, what would be your dream? (To be a gourmet cook and a rock climber, a talented singer and a deep-sea diver, an Olympic track star and an astronaut, . . .)
- What else might this bumper sticker be talking about?
- In what ways does Jesus ask you to take up your cross and follow Him?
- As Jesus obeyed God by going to the cross, so you need to obey God even when it's hard. Have you had to do that lately? When? Maybe that's *real* cross training!

"Father God created mother earth."

Hard. Any length trip. Ages 7 and up.

Fill in the blanks to make up your own personal bumper sticker:
  "Sister (name) (verb) brother (name)."
  For instance: "Sister (Kristen) (jostled) Brother (Vincent)."
  Talk about the sticker "Father God created mother earth."

- God *did* create the earth—check out Genesis chapters 1 and 2—but where did this "mother earth" idea come from?
- Is this phrase suggesting that the earth is a spiritual being, like God the Father?
- Or could it be trying to put the "mother earth" thinking in the right perspective?

- It could be thought of in different ways. What's your opinion? Why? Knowing God's Word helps you identify things that are misleading or false.

"Life is short. Pray hard!"

Moderate. Any length trip. All ages.

Think of bumper stickers similar to this one. For example, "Life is slow. Live fast!" or "Life is long. Go on vacation."
- What things do you hope to accomplish in your lifetime?
- What would be some BIG dreams that you would love to have come true, if possible?
- How could you begin to take small steps toward those dreams?

"I'm fat; you're ugly. I can diet."

Moderate. Any length trip. All ages.

Of course, this is a joke. Is it funny? Why do you—or don't you—think so?
- Can you think of some bumper stickers that would be more complimentary?
- What if there were bumper stickers in heaven on the streets of gold. How would they be different from this one?
- Think of some other "heavenly" bumper stickers, for example, "I ♥ my mansion," "I stop for Bible characters," "Joy on board."

"How's my driving? Call 1-800-YOU-JERK."

Moderate. Any length trip. All ages.

- What do you think about this sticker?
- Who are they calling a jerk? The driver or you?
- Would your parents want someone evaluating their driving? Why or why not?
- How should Christians try to drive? Why do you think so?

Make up other 1-800 numbers that could become good or humorous bumper stickers. Such as, "If you can read this, call 1-800-TOO-CLOSE."

Bible
Bafflers

Mystery Challenges

Any length trip. All ages. Note: Someone other than the driver needs to read the rhymes.

Read the following rhyme mysteries to your children and see if they can guess who or what the mystery is about. Pause briefly between the sentences to build the suspense. Older children might be able to guess the answers before you get to the end; however, younger children will want the chance to guess after the whole rhyme has been read.

After doing a few, see if you can make up one about a family member, a friend, something in the car, or something outside that you pass every day on the way to school.

1. *(Hard)*
   I'll tell a little story all about a man named—Oh!
   I'd better not tell you his name, for then you'll surely know.
   This man, he sure did travel his share far 'round the world.
   His past was not so pretty—many lives he did uncurl!
   Till one day he was walking on a hot and dusty road,
   The brightest of lights did shine 'til he dropped his heavy load.
   Then a voice was heard from heaven with great thundering sound.
   "Stop doin' what you're doin', man, to evil you've been bound!
   You change your ways, right now. You see I want this world to know
   That I can change the hardest hearts and make them overflow."
   The moral of this story is that God *did* change that man.
   He turned his life around and worked to change that sinful land.
   The words he wrote can now be read in your Bible and mine.
   So don't lose hope in what you see—God's in control just fine.
   Who was this man?

2. *(Easy)*
   I am meek and I am mild.
   I follow like a little child.
   One day I strayed from all the rest.

My master found me—he's the best!
I do not argue or complain.
I'll even stand out in the rain.
Many thank me for their coat.
I'm in the songs that David wrote.
Yes all, like me, have gone astray.
Trust God to lead you in His way.
What am I?

3. *(Hard)*

If ever 'twas a man who lived and saw the strangest things
It was this priest in exile, who did more than simply sing.
The hand of God came on him in a mighty storm one
    day.
Then wind and fire surrounded him—the voice of God
    did say,
"You'll have to preach the truth—I need your voice out in
    the street."
Then suddenly a scroll appeared and God said, "This
    you'll eat."
One day out in a valley some dry bones did come to life.
Whoever would have seen it would have surely died of
    fright.
To prophesy and prophesy was what this man would do
For God had chosen him to tell of all the troubling news.
Who was this man?

4. *(Easy)*

Out of me comes evil.
Out of me comes love.
I'm at the very core of things,
E'en the Father up above.
Sometimes I will melt,
And other times I'll break.
When afraid I'll move real fast.
I always am awake.
Do not lose me, or you'll find
Your life gets dark and sad.
Love your God with all of me,
And then you will be glad.
What am I?

5. *(Moderate)*
   Happy days are here again; I can't believe it's true.
   To see my father's smile again and hear his "I love you."
   Well, I admit it was God's will that all this came to be—
   A coat, a pit, and ill intent from my dear family.
   My brothers didn't mean such harm, I really do believe.
   Yet one mistake changed everything, they now can
       plainly see.
   Through famine, illness, hungry days God worked His plan
       through time.
   Do you know just who I am from this here little rhyme?

ANSWERS TO MYSTERY CHALLENGES:

1. Paul
2. Sheep
3. Ezekiel
4. Heart
5. Joseph

Equations of the Bible

Any length trip. Ages 7 and up.

The numbers in the following equations stand for something in the Bible. The initials on the right side of the equation are the first letters of the words of what that something is. Emphasize the right side of the equation, reading the letters clearly and distinctly. For example,

a. 12=D of J "Twelve equals **D of J**. What do the D and J stand for?"
   Answer: 12 Disciples of Jesus
b. *(M)* 6=D of C
c. *(E)* 3=P of G
d. *(E)* 39=B of the OT
e. *(M)* 12=T of I
f. *(E)* 30=P of S
g. *(M)* 10=C in S
h. *(E)* 27=B of the NT
i. *(M)* 40=Y in the W
j. *(M)* 1=W of S
k. *(H)* 7=T around the C or 7=T around J
l. *(H)* 2=CC of the W

Now have some fun making up your own family equations, such as 4=P in OF (4 People in Our Family), or 2=C we O (2 Cats we Own).

ANSWERS FOR EQUATIONS OF THE BIBLE:

a. 12 Disciples of Jesus
b. 6 Days of Creation
c. 3 Persons of God
d. 39 Books of the Old Testament
e. 12 Tribes of Israel
f. 30 Pieces of Silver
g. 10 Commandments in Stone
h. 27 Books of the New Testament
i. 40 Years in the Wilderness
j. 1 Way of Salvation
k. 7 Times around the City (Jericho)
l. 2 Copper coins of the Widow

Follow the Clue Trivia

Any length trip. All ages. Note: Someone other than the driver needs to read the clues.

Give children one clue at a time from the mysteries that follow and allow them time to guess at what the answer might be. Encourage them to talk together about it. Only go on to the next clue when they really need it to continue their guesses. Three clues are given, from hard to easy, to reveal the answer.

Add fun by making up additional clue questions for each other about personal things, such as your school, church, sports, your grandparents, friends, favorite television shows, family books.

1. *(M)* Who am I?
   Clue #1: My father was over 500 years old when my brothers and I were born.
   Clue #2: My father received a command from God. If I didn't know how to use a saw before that, I sure found out quickly.
   Clue #3: My brothers are Ham and Japheth.
2. *(E)* Who am I?
   Clue #1: Mary came to tell me that an angel visited her with amazing news.

Clue #2: My son was beheaded at the request of Herodias.
Clue #3: My husband wasn't able to speak during my pregnancy.

3. *(H)* Who am I?
   Clue #1: I once made an image of gold 90-feet high.
   Clue #2: I once had to live and eat grass like a cow to teach me a lesson.
   Clue #3: Daniel interpreted my troubling dreams and I learned to trust in his God.

4. *(M)* Who am I?
   Clue #1: Paul was a good friend of mine.
   Clue #2: I have more education than many of my friends, and in fact, people come to me when they're sick.
   Clue #3: I didn't sign my name, but people have figured out that I wrote the book of Acts.

5. *(E)* Who am I?
   Clue #1: I allowed Satan to tempt me and later regretted it.
   Clue #2: The chief priests used money I returned to them to buy a potter's field.
   Clue #3: I am well known for a kiss.

6. *(M)* Who am I?
   Clue #1: Someone visited me at the threshing floor one night.
   Clue #2: I am referred to as a kinsman-redeemer.
   Clue #3: My story is told in the book of Ruth.

7. *(M)* Who am I?
   Clue #1: My sons wrestled with each other all of their lives.
   Clue #2: I gave birth to twins.
   Clue #3: I wrongly helped one son deceive his father.

8. *(E)* Who am I?
   Clue #1: Two angels visited me at my home in Sodom.
   Clue #2: Abraham gave me the choice of land that I wanted.
   Clue #3: My wife became a pillar of salt when she looked back.

9. *(E)* What am I?
   Clue #1: You can find me in the book of Exodus.
   Clue #2: I was given to the people through Moses.
   Clue #3: I was first written on stone on Mt. Sinai.

10. *(M)* What am I?
    Clue #1: I was made of melted jewelry.
    Clue #2: Moses got so mad when he saw me that he threw

God's tablets down and broke them to pieces.
Clue #3: I am no god, but the people acted like I was.

ANSWERS FOR FOLLOW THE CLUE TRIVIA:
1. Shem, the son of Noah from whom the Israelites descended
2. Elizabeth
3. King Nebuchadnezzar
4. Luke
5. Judas Iscariot
6. Boaz
7. Rebekah
8. Lot
9. The Ten Commandments
10. The golden calf

Truth or Consequences?

Any length trip. All ages. Note: Someone other than the driver needs to read the questions.

The following questions deal with scenes from the Bible where the truth was difficult or dangerous to give. Read the statement a Bible character *could* have said—but didn't—and have your children guess who it was. Some of the characters lied and paid the consequences. Others told the truth and experienced other consequences. Talk about the choices each character made and their results. What would the consequences have been if they *had* made these statements?

1. *(M)* Who could have said, "I have no idea why these waves are crashing our boat"?
2. *(E)* Who could have said, "Father, we lied to you about your other son"?
3. *(M)* Who could have said, "Sure, we'll bow to the golden image—no problem!"?
4. *(M)* Who could have said, "Eli, I can't remember what God said about you"?
5. *(H)* Who could have avoided being stoned by saying, "I was just telling stories. None of it's really true"?
6. *(E)* Who could have said three times, "Yes, I know Him. He is the Son of God"?

7. *(E)* Who could have said, "Father, I've saved the money you gave me in a bank. I just decided it was time to come back home"?
8. *(H)* Who could have said, "I am closer than a sister; I am his wife"?
9. *(E)* Who could have said, "Father, I am pretending to be my brother"?
10. *(E)* Who could have said, "Someone is actually paying me money to build this boat, so don't laugh at me"?
11. *(E)* Who could have said, "Thanks for coming over, Jesus—it's been great. But I can't give back all the money I've taken!"?

Can you think of other times a Bible character might have been tempted to avoid the truth? Or can you think of a Bible character who told the truth with bad results?

ANSWERS FOR TRUTH OR CONSEQUENCES?

1. Jonah (Jonah 1:12 tells what really happened).
2. Jacob's sons regarding what they did to Joseph (Genesis 37:28–32).
3. Shadrach, Meshach, and Abednego (Daniel 3:18).
4. Samuel (1 Samuel 3:18).
5. Stephen (Acts 7:54–58).
6. Peter, rather than denying Jesus before the rooster crowed (John 18:27).
7. The Prodigal Son (Luke 15:18).
8. Sarah and Rebekah both had the chance to say this (Genesis 20:2; 26:7).
9. Jacob (Genesis 27:22–24).
10. Noah (Genesis 6:22).
11. Zacchaeus (Luke 19:8).

What *Does Not* Belong?

Any length trip. All ages. Note: Someone other than the driver needs to read the lists.

Read these lists to your children and see if they can pick out the item that does not belong with the others in each group. They get a bonus if they can say why it doesn't fit. (Adding the "why" makes it harder.)

1. *(E)* Fork, spoon, plate, napkin, knife, thank–you note.

2. *(M)* Genesis, Nehemiah, Malachi, Revelation, Exodus, Psalms.
3. *(M)* Peter, Judas, John, Aladdin, James, Matthew, David.
4. *(E)* Joy, patience, love, peace, kindness, baldness.
5. *(E)* Saul, David, Peter pumpkin eater, Solomon, Herod, Ahab.
6. *(M)* Healing the sick, resurrecting Lazarus, changing water to wine, walking on the water, feeding the multitude, calling fire down from heaven.
7. *(M)* Lyre, harp, harmonica, trumpet, cymbals, flute.
8. *(H)* Frankincense, perfume, myrrh, spices, dead fish, pizza.
9. *(M)* Stealing, gossiping, cleaning, murdering, taking God's name in vain.
10. *(M)* Mary, Martha, Priscilla, Elizabeth, Lydia, Twila.
11. *(E)* Oceans, people, plants, Gameboy, fish, little red hen.
12. *(E)* Mickey Mouse, Donald Duck, Goofy, Bugs Bunny, Michael Jordan.
13. *(M)* Revelation, Psalms, Titus, Hebrews, Romans, Mark.
14. *(H)* Jericho, Jerusalem, Sodom, Philadelphia, Damascus, Chicago.
15. *(H)* Bread, fish, milk, waffles, manna, grapes.
16. *(E)* Sea of Galilee, well, stream, temple pool, faucet, rain.
17. *(E)* Wine, bread, disciples, towel, feet, supper, Oil of Olay.
18. *(E)* Canaanites, Midianites, Calamity–ites, Philistines, Egyptians, Israelites.
19. *(M)* Tents, Israelites, pillar of fire, Moses, heat, sunscreen.
20. *(M)* Animals, sons, temple, Noah, wife, daughters-in-law, two turtledoves.

See if you can come up with some of your own. For example: Think about names of family members, things in your house, teachers at your school, Bible stories, games on your shelf at home, things you got for Christmas last year, things your parents say, etc.

ANSWERS FOR WHAT DOES NOT BELONG:
1. Thank–you note (not part of a table setting)
2. Revelation (the only New Testament book listed)
3. Trick question with two answers: David and Aladdin (not one of the twelve disciples)
4. Baldness (not a fruit of the Spirit)
5. Peter pumpkin eater (not a king)
6. Calling fire down from heaven (not a miracle of Jesus)

7. Harmonica (not an instrument mentioned in the Bible)
8. Dead fish (doesn't smell good)
9. Cleaning (not warned against in the Bible)
10. Twila (not a woman of the Bible, the New Testament in particular)
11. Gameboy (not one of the things God created in the six days of creation—Genesis 1)
12. Michael Jordan (the only real person)
13. Psalms (the only Old Testament book listed)
14. Chicago (not a biblical town)
15. Waffles (not a biblical food)
16. Faucet (not a biblical water source)
17. Oil of Olay (not a part of the Last Supper)
18. Calamity–ites (not a real group of people in the Bible)
19. Sunscreen (no sunscreen was available during 40 years in the wilderness)
20. The temple (wasn't in the ark with Noah)

Headlines

Any length trip. All ages. Note: Someone other than the driver needs to read the headlines.

Read the following headlines of events found in the Bible to your children. See if they know what the story is and whether it is found in the Old or New Testament.

1. *(E)* Nothing, Words, then Many Somethings
2. *(E)* Tons of Water1!
3. *(M)* Locust-Eating, Camel-Hair-Wearing Preacher
4. *(M)* Unwilling Brick Makers
5. *(M)* Great Walls of Water!
6. *(E)* A Star Announces the News
7. *(E)* Small Seed Makes It Big
8. *(M)* Bad Hair Day!
9. *(E)* Shepherd with a Crown
10. *(E)* A Peewee, a Stone, and a Thud
11. *(E)* Words in Stone
12. *(H)* A Blinding "About Face!"
13. *(H)* Home at Last; But Never Been There Before
14. *(E)* Wise Men Visit King
15. *(M)* The Great Wall Crash

16. *(H)* Trips with a Purpose
17. *(M)* Ezekiel Sees Surprising Stuff!
18. *(M)* House for God Built
19. *(M)* The Greatest Sacrifice Ever!
20. *(E)* A Promise Signed in Colors
21. *(M)* "Beach" House Bobs Away!
22. *(E)* Colorful Coat Causes Cruelty
23. *(E)* Palm Branches Spread Before Him
24. *(M)* Project Abandoned Due to Communication Problems
25. *(H)* A Walk with a Mysterious Stranger
26. *(M)* Cut Off Ear Repaired
27. *(E)* Frogs, Gnats, Boils, Hail, Death, Blood, . . .
28. *(E)* Queen Risks Death for Her People
29. *(E)* Animal Skin Wins Birthright
30. *(M)* Viper Not So Venomous

Can you think of others to stump your family?

ANSWERS FOR HEADLINES

"(Old)" and "(New)" indicate which Testament the story appears in.

1. Creation (Old)
2. Flood (Old)
3. John the Baptist (New)
4. Israelite slaves in Egypt (Old)
5. Parting of the Red Sea (Old)
6. Jesus is born (New)
7. Parable of the mustard seed (New)
8. Samson (Old)
9. King David (Old)
10. Goliath killed (Old)
11. The Ten Commandments (Old)
12. Paul's conversion (New)
13. Promised Land (Old)
14. Magi visit Herod (New)
15. Jericho walls fall (Old)
16. Paul's missionary journeys (New)
17. Ezekiel's visions (Old)
18. Solomon built the temple (Old)
19. Jesus' death/life (New)
20. First rainbow (Old)
21. Parable of house built on sand (New)

22. Joseph (Old)
23. Jesus in Jerusalem (New)
24. Tower of Babel (Old)
25. Jesus on road to Emmaus (New)
26. Jesus healed the soldier's ear at His arrest (New)
27. 10 plagues of Egypt (Old)
28. Queen Esther (Old)
29. Jacob (Old)
30. Paul bitten, but not hurt (New)

BIBLE LEBBI*

Moderate. Trips 30 minutes or longer. Ages 7 and up. Best for children who read well. You'll need paper and pens.

What's LEBBI? It's BIBLE scrambled up. Use paper and pens to unscramble the following words. Work together or have a contest to see who can unscramble the biblical words first.

1. VELO	14. CRAFISCEI
2. DSOMIW	15. SERUPOP
3. SUESJ	16. CEETNIAP
4. THRUT	17. COIJEER
5. RLYOG	18. TRISHC
6. TIRIPSLAU	19. THREAF
7. NGODOSES	20. NEAM
8. VEESR	21. YEAPRR
9. ACEEP	22. MEAPLEX
10. RHEAS	23. ROWELLFO
11. CREAG	24. LEERBEIV
12. ENSUSSTHOERIG	25. DRAPASIE
13. TOEDDEV	26. LINGASTVEER

Children can also play this by challenging one another with a list of words that they have scrambled for themselves. Exchange lists of 10 or 20 words.

ANSWERS TO BIBLE LEBBI:

1. LOVE	14. SACRIFICE
2. WISDOM	15. PURPOSE
3. JESUS	16. PATIENCE
4. TRUTH	17. REJOICE
5. GLORY	18. CHRIST
6. SPIRITUAL	19. FATHER

7. GOODNESS
8. SERVE
9. PEACE
10. SHARE
11. GRACE
12. RIGHTEOUSNESS
13. DEVOTED

20. AMEN or NAME
21. PRAYER
22. EXAMPLE
23. FOLLOWER
24. BELIEVER
25. PARADISE
26. EVERLASTING

Sounds Like

*Any length trip. All ages. Note: Someone other than the driver
needs to read the phrases.*

See if you can stump your children with these Bible phrases.
The word (or words) in italics is to be replaced with the proper
word that sounds like that word (or words). Your children will
have to use their imagination. Be a little silly.

Example: *Fount* your *dressings* = Count your blessings.

1. *(E)* Answer to *hair*
2. *(E)* Blessed are the *door*
3. *(M)* In *pretendance* of *tea*
4. *(M)* *Moo* of *brittle* faith
5. *(E)* *Met* the *brittle* children *hum*
6. *(E)* I *fell shoe* the truth
7. *(M)* *Chew* not *flurry*
8. *(E)* Do not *free* a *braid*
9. *(E)* *Swallow flea*
10. *(E)* Do not *squeal*
11. *(H)* The *bend rhymes*
12. *(M)* *Tour* faith has *wheeled* you
13. *(E)* Let my *steeple flow*
14. *(E)* *Glove* your *labor*
15. *(E)* *Row* in *fleece*
16. *(E)* *Rumble* yourself
17. *(E)* Let your *sight dine*
18. *(M)* *Flew* to *smothers*
19. *(M)* *Plead* my *bleep*
20. *(H)* *Space* and *fleece* to you

For more "Sounds Like" fun, make up some additional phrases with favorite or family sayings often heard in your household.

ANSWERS TO SOUNDS LIKE:
1. Answer to prayer
2. Blessed are the poor
3. In remembrance of me
4. You of little faith
5. Let the little children come
6. I tell you the truth
7. Do not worry
8. Do not be afraid
9. Follow me
10. Do not steal
11. The end times
12. Your faith has healed you
13. Let my people go
14. Love your neighbor
15. Go in peace
16. Humble yourself
17. Let your light shine
18. Do to others
19. Feed my sheep
20. Grace and peace to you

Lessons from the Sermon on the Mount

Any length trip. All ages. Note: Someone other than the driver needs to read the questions.

This famous sermon of Jesus is recorded in Matthew 5–7. See how quickly your children can answer these questions from this important message.

1. *(E)* Blessed are the poor in spirit, for theirs is the kingdom of _____.
2. *(M)* Those who mourn will be _____.
3. *(M)* The meek will inherit _____ _____.
4. *(M)* Those who hunger and thirst for righteousness will be _____.
5. *(E)* The pure in heart will see _____.
6. *(H)* _____ will be called sons of God.
7. *(M)* What two things are you to be? You are (something to taste) and (something to see).

8. *(H)* Anyone who breaks God's commandments and teaches others to will be called this.
9. *(E)* True or False: Jesus teaches people to settle matters quickly with those they have troubles with.
10. *(E)* What is NOT a way to love your enemies? a. Praying for them, b. Seeking to work out disagreements, c. Repeating unkind rumors about them, or d. Giving them your coat.
11. *(E)* Jesus encourages gifts to the needy to be given how? a. In secret, b. Announcing them with trumpets, or c. In very small amounts.
12. *(E)* Who sees what you do in secret?
13. *(M)* True or False: Your Father knows what you need only after you ask Him.
14. *(H)* The eye is the _____ of the body.
15. *(M)* How much time can you add to your life by worrying? a. One hour, b. Not a single hour, or c. It's hard to tell—no one's been able to measure it.
16. *(H)* True or False: Judge others critically then God will judge you very easily.
17. *(M)* What happens to the person who knocks?
18. *(E)* Is the gate that leads to life wide or narrow?
19. *(M)* Both trees and people are recognized by what?

ANSWERS FOR SERMON ON THE MOUNT, FOUND IN MATTHEW:
1. Heaven (5:3)
2. Comforted (5:4)
3. The earth (5:5)
4. Filled (5:6)
5. God (5:8)
6. Peacemakers (5:9)
7. Salt (of the earth) and light (of the world) (5:13–14)
8. Least (in the kingdom of heaven) (5:19)
9. True (5:25)
10. c. Repeating unkind rumors about them.
11. a. In secret (6:4)
12. The Father (6:4, 6)
13. False (6:8)
14. Lamp (6:22)
15. b. Not a single hour (6:27)
16. False (7:1, 2)
17. The door will be opened for him or her. (7:8)

18. Narrow (7:13–14)
19. Their fruit (7:16)

What TIME Is It?

Any length trip. All ages. Note: Someone other than the driver needs to read the questions.

See how well your children know your Bible "times." You can make it more challenging if you ask them to tell whether the reference comes from the Old or the New Testament.

1. *(E)* How many times should you forgive others?
2. *(E)* Who will appear a second time?
3. *(H)* There is a time for everything where?
4. *(M)* What times do friends love?
5. *(M)* Jesus sat at the Samaritan woman's well at "about the sixth hour." About what time is that in today's way of telling time?
6. *(E)* Jesus walked on the water at what time of day?
7. *(M)* What were the disciples called for the first time at Antioch?
8. *(E)* Did Jesus die on the cross in the daytime or in the nighttime?
9. *(M)* Who knows the day and hour that Christ will return?
10. *(E)* What time of day did the Lord send the plague of the firstborn upon Egypt (the Passover event)?
11. *(E)* On the seventh day how many times did the people have to march around Jericho?

ANSWERS FOR WHAT TIME IS IT?

1. 77 times (Matthew 18:22)
2. Jesus (Hebrews 9:28)
3. Under heaven (Ecclesiastes 3:1)
4. At all times (Proverbs 17:17)
5. Noon (John 4:6) (The "first hour" is 7:00 A.M., so the sixth is noon.)
6. Evening, after dark, or at night (John 6:16–19)
7. Christians (Acts 11:26)
8. Daytime—around 3:00 in the afternoon. Although the whole land had turned dark since about noon. (Matthew 27:45–46)
9. Only the Father (Matthew 24:36)

10. Midnight (Exodus 12:29)
11. Seven times (Joshua 6:4)

Biblemania Showdown

Trips longer than 15 minutes. All ages.

Let one child be the "host" for all the clues included in one category. The answers are right below the clues, so the "host" should not let other children see the book. (Children of all ages can answer the questions but "hosts" must be able to read.)

The "host" informs the other children of the category, and then reads the clue. The clue is really the correct answer to a question. The other children need to figure out what the question would be and give the correct response in the form of a question. "What is _____?" or "Who is _____?" This is tricky at first, but lots of fun. After getting a correct answer, the "host" goes on to the next clue in that category. When there is a new category, the children choose a new host. Here are a couple of examples to read to give everyone an idea of how to make the responses into questions:

Category: Kings
   Clue: This king was given the job of building the temple.
   Correct response: "Who is King Solomon?"

Category: Prophets
   Clue: The book named after this prophet contains the most words of any book in the Bible.
   Correct response: "Who is Jeremiah?"

Okay, have the children select the first "host" and go for it!

Category: Kings—*(M)*
1. *Clue:* He was found hiding in the baggage when they made him king (1 Samuel 10:22).
   Correct response: "Who is Saul?"
2. *Clue:* He was once the best friend of Jonathan, Saul's son.
   Correct response: "Who is David?"
3. *Clue:* He is the king who had a wicked wife named Jezebel.
   Correct response: "Who is Ahab?"
4. *Clue:* This king was given no golden crown but was mocked with a crown of thorns.
   Correct response: "Who is Jesus?"

Category: Prophets—*(H)*
1. *Clue:* The great prophet whose name means, "The Lord saves."
   Correct response: "Who is Isaiah?"
2. *Clue:* The prophet who saw weird creatures and wheels with eyes.
   Correct response: "Who is Ezekiel?"
3. *Clue:* This prophet and his friends requested the vegetarian menu.
   Correct response: "Who is Daniel?"
4. *Clue:* A prophet who loved his wife, Gomer, despite her lack of commitment to him.
   Correct response: "Who is Hosea?"

Category: Things that Jesus healed—*(E)*
1. *Clue:* Jesus asked the man to stretch this out to Him because it was shriveled.
   Correct response: "What is a hand?" (Matthew 12:13)
2. *Clue:* A woman was healed from this when she touched Jesus in a crowd.
   Correct response: "What is bleeding?" (Mark 5:29)
3. *Clue:* Jesus told the ten men with this disease to go show themselves to the priests.
   Correct response: "What is leprosy?" (Luke 17:12–14)
4. *Clue:* Jesus used some of His own saliva to make mud to heal these.
   Correct response: "What are eyes?" (John 9:6)

Category: Letters of Paul—*(M)*
1. *Clue:* This letter was written to Christians in a large city and comes after the book of Acts in the Bible.
   Correct response: "What is Romans?"
2. *Clue:* This letter includes the famous "love chapter."
   Correct response: "What is 1 Corinthians?"
3. *Clue:* This letter, written from prison, thanks the people of Philippi for the gift they sent Paul in Rome.
   Correct response: "What is Philippians?"
4. *Clue:* Paul writes two letters to this person whom he calls his "true son in the faith."
   Correct response: "Who is Timothy?"

Category: Years in the wilderness—*(E)*
1. *Clue:* He was chosen by God to be the leader of the Israelites as they left Egypt and traveled in the wilderness.
   Correct response: "Who is Moses?"
2. *Clue:* God gave this meat to the Israelites when they complained.
   Correct response: "What is quail?" (Exodus 16:13)
3. *Clue:* This is the name of the container in which God's commandments were placed.
   Correct response: "What is the ark (or ark of the Testimony)?" (Exodus 25:21, 22)
4. *Clue:* He was the new leader who led the people into the Promised Land after 40 years in the wilderness.
   Correct response: "Who is Joshua?" (Joshua 1:1, 2)

Category: Baby steps—*(E)*
1. *Clue:* This baby's birth was announced to shepherds by angels.
   Correct response: "Who is Jesus?"
2. *Clue:* This baby jumped in his mother's womb.
   Correct response: "Who is John the Baptist?"
3. *Clue:* This baby was found by Pharaoh's daughter.
   Correct response: "Who is Moses?"
4. *Clue:* This baby was a twin who grabbed on to the heel of the firstborn.
   Correct response: "Who is Jacob?" (Genesis 25:26)

Category: Proverbs—*(H)*
1. *Clue:* Proverbs says *this* goes before destruction.
   Correct response: "What is pride?" (Proverbs 16:18)
2. *Clue:* This kind of hair is the splendor of the old.
   Correct response: "What is gray hair?" (Proverbs 20:29)
3. *Clue:* If you have a happy heart, it will make your face look this way.
   Correct response: "What is cheerful?" (Proverbs 15:13)
4. *Clue:* Even a child is known by this.
   Correct response: "What are actions?" (Proverbs 20:11)

Category: The disciple whom Jesus loved . . . and his book—*(M)*
1. *Clue:* This disciple whom Jesus loved wrote one of the four Gospels.
   Correct response: "Who is John?"

2. *Clue:* The story of Jesus raising this man to life is found only in John's gospel.
Correct response: "Who is Lazarus?"
3. *Clue:* The disciple whom Jesus loved took this woman into his home.
Correct response: "Who is Jesus' mother (or Mary, the mother of Jesus)?" (John 19:27)
4. *Clue:* This man, whose name begins with the sound of a five-cent coin, asked Jesus about what it meant to be born again.
Correct response: "Who is Nicodemus?" (John 3:4)

Category: Commandments—*(E)*
1. *Clue:* You are violating this command if you shoplift.
Correct response: "What is 'You shall not steal'?"
2. *Clue:* This word means to want something that someone else has.
Correct response: "What is covet?"
3. *Clue:* If money, or television, or sports, or anything else is more important to you than God is, look out for this commandment.
Correct response: "What is 'You shall have no other gods before Me'?"
4. *Clue:* You do this well if you are obedient and respectful.
Correct response: "What is 'Honor your father and mother'?"

Category: Things in the temple—*(M/H)*
1. *Clue:* There were ten of these made of pure gold to hold the lamps.
Correct response: "What are lamp stands?"
2. *Clue:* The bread of the Presence was placed on this.
Correct response: "What is the table?"
3. *Clue:* This room was reserved for the ark of the covenant.
Correct response: "What is the Most Holy Place (or the Holy of Holies)?"
4. *Clue:* You use this to mix things in, but the priests may have used it to dip fingers in for water.
Correct response: "What is a bowl?"

Category: Things in the garden—*(M)*
1. *Clue:* Four of these watered the Garden of Eden.
Correct response: "What are rivers?" (Genesis 2:10–14)
2. *Clue:* God made this from the dust of the ground.

Correct response: "What is man?" or "Who is Adam?"(Genesis 2:7)
3. *Clue:* This tree has the same name as a Milton Bradley game.
   Correct response: "What is life (or the Tree of Life)?"
4. *Clue:* This precious metal is used for making wedding rings.
   Correct response: "What is gold?" (Genesis 2:11, 12)

Category: Colors—*(E)*
1. *Clue:* This is the color of the robe that was placed on Jesus to mock Him.
   Correct response: "What is purple?" (Mark 15:17)
2. *Clue:* This is the sea that the Israelites crossed to escape Pharaoh.
   Correct response: "What is the Red Sea?"
3. *Clue:* A color often used to describe something spotless and pure.
   Correct response: "What is white?"
4. *Clue:* The Lord, my Shepherd, makes me to lie down here.
   Correct response: "What are green pastures?" (Psalm 23:2)

Category: Gotta have faith—*(H)*
1. *Clue:* If your faith is as small as this, you can still do great things.
   Correct response: "What is a mustard seed?" (Luke 17:6)
2. *Clue:* Abraham's faith was credited to him as this.
   Correct response: "What is righteousness?" (Romans 4:9)
3. *Clue:* This is a good fight.
   Correct response: "What is the fight of faith?" (1 Timothy 6:12)
4. *Clue:* This is what faith without deeds is.
   Correct response: "What is dead?" (James 2:26)

Category: Foolishness—*(H)*
1. *Clue:* This man foolishly built a house here.
   Correct response: "What is on the sand?" (Matthew 7:26)
2. *Clue:* He who trusts in himself is this.
   Correct response: "What is a fool?" (Proverbs 28:26)
3. *Clue:* Fools hate this, but it is necessary for parents to do it.
   Correct response: "What is discipline?" (Proverbs 1:7)
4. *Clue:* A fool says in his _____, "There is no God."
   Correct response: "What is a heart?" (Psalm 14:1)

Category: Plants—*(M/H)*

1. *Clue:* This type of plant grew up to provide Jonah with shade.
   Correct response: "What is a vine?" (Jonah 4:6)
2. *Clue:* This is what the dove brought back to Noah that showed that the waters had gone down.
   Correct response: "What is an olive leaf?" (Genesis 8:11)
3. *Clue:* This tree was the only tree in the garden that Adam was not allowed to eat from.
   Correct response: "What is the Tree of the Knowledge of Good and Evil?" (Genesis 2:17)
4. *Clue:* This plant was used to lift the sponge to Jesus' lips.
   Correct response: "What is a hyssop plant?" (John 19:29)

Category: Familiar sayings—*(H)*

1. *Clue:* The phrase "by the skin of my teeth" was said by this man in despair.
   Correct response: "Who is Job?" (Job 19:20)
2. *Clue:* Jesus used a saying like this that might be thought of as an animal masquerade party.
   Correct response: "What is a wolf in sheep's clothing?" (Matthew 7:15)
3. *Clue:* "Woe to me" was said by this prophet whose name begins with a vowel.
   Correct response: "Who is Isaiah?" (Isaiah 6:5)
4. *Clue:* This familiar phrase comes from an occasion when Jesus said that if [these men] follow each other, both will fall into a pit.
   Correct response: "What is the blind leading the blind?" (Matthew 15:14)

Feel free to make up your own categories with clues. For example, family rules, chores around the house, things to find at garage sales.

Topical Index

Try These Other Heritage Builders Resources!

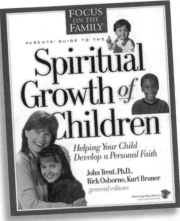

Parents' Guide to the Spiritual Growth of Children

Building a foundation of faith in your children can be easy–and fun!–with help from the *Parents' Guide to the Spiritual Growth of Children*. Through simple and practical advice, this comprehensive guide shows you how to build a spiritual training plan for your family and it explains what to teach your children at different ages.

Joy Ride!

Use your drive time to teach your kids how faith can be part of everyday life with *Joy Ride!* A wonderful resource for parents, this book features activities, puzzles, games and discussion starters to help get your kids thinking about—and living out—what they believe.

My Time With God, Volume 2

Kids will see that quiet times with God can be both inspiring and fun with *My Time With God, Volume 2.* Like the successful first volume, this Heritage Builders paperback shows kids ages 8 to 12 how to link up with God and His Word through 150 days' worth of fun facts, trivia, prayer starters, and much more.

Heritage Builders™

Helping You Build a Family of Faith

Bedtime Blessings, Volume 2

Over the course of 100 evenings, you can deepen your child's relationship with God—and yourself—with John Trent's ***Bedtime Blessings, Volume 2.*** Like the best-selling author's successful first volume, this Heritage Builders hardcover is filled with stories, activities, games, and bedtime prayers for kids ages 7 and under.

Extending Your Heritage

Extending Your Heritage gives practical ways to influence your family, be a role model to young people who lack proper role models, and give children and young people a heritage through your influence on their lives. The paperback also encourages all Christian adults to reach beyond their own families by volunteering and encouraging young neighbors.

• • •

Visit our Heritage Builders Web site! Log on to
www.heritagebuilders.com to discover new resources,
sample activities, and ideas to help you pass on a spiritual heritage.
To request any of these resources, simply call Focus on the Family at
1-800-A-FAMILY (1-800-232-6459) or in Canada, call 1-800-661-9800.
Or send your request to Focus on the Family, Colorado Springs, CO
80995. In Canada, write Focus on the Family, P.O. Box 9800,
Stn. Terminal, Vancouver, B.C. V6B 4G3.

Heritage™
Builders
Helping You Build a Family of Faith

Welcome to the Family!

Heritage
Builders™

Helping You Build a Family of Faith

We hope you've enjoyed this book. Heritage Builders was founded in 1995 by three fathers with a passion for the next generation. As a new ministry of Focus on the Family, Heritage Builders strives to equip, train and motivate parents to become intentional about building a strong spiritual heritage.

It's quite a challenge for busy parents to find ways to build a spiritual foundation for their families—especially in a way they enjoy and understand. Through activities and participation, children can learn biblical truth in a way they can understand, enjoy—and *remember*.

Passing along a heritage of Christian faith to your family is a parent's highest calling. Heritage Builders' goal is to encourage and empower you in this great mission with practical resources and inspiring ideas that really work— and help your children develop a lasting love for God.

***

How To Reach Us

For more information, visit our Heritage Builders Web site! Log on to **www.heritagebuilders.com** to discover new resources, sample activities, and ideas to help you pass on a spiritual heritage. To request any of these resources, simply call Focus on the Family at 1-800-A-FAMILY (1-800-232-6459) or in Canada, call 1-800-661-9800. Or send your request to Focus on the Family, Colorado Springs, CO 80995. In Canada, write Focus on the Family, P.O. Box 9800, Stn. Terminal, Vancouver, B.C. V6B 4G3

To learn more about Focus on the Family or to find out if there is an associate office in your country, please visit www. family.org

We'd love to hear from you!

Every family has a heritage—a spiritual, emotional, and social legacy passed from one generation to the next. There are four main areas we at Heritage Builders recommend parents consider as they plan to pass their faith to their children:

Family Fragrance

Every family's home has a fragrance. Heritage Builders encourages parents to create a home environment that fosters a sweet, Christ-centered AROMA of love through Affection, Respect, Order, Merriment, and Affirmation.

Family Traditions

Whether you pass down stories, beliefs and/or customs, traditions can help you establish a special identity for your family. Heritage Builders encourages parents to set special "milestones" for their children to help guide them and move them through their spiritual development.

Family Compass

Parents have the unique task of setting standards for normal, healthy living through their attitudes, actions and beliefs. Heritage Builders encourages parents to give their children the moral navigation tools they need to succeed on the roads of life.

Family Moments

Creating special, teachable moments with their children is one of a parent's most precious and sometimes, most difficult responsibilities. Heritage Builders encourages parents to capture little moments throughout the day to teach and impress values, beliefs, and biblical principles onto their children.

We look forward to standing alongside you as you seek to impart the Lord's care and wisdom to the next generation—to your children.

Heritage
Builders™

Helping You Build a Family of Faith

LIGHT wave

building Christian faith in families

Lightwave Publishing is one of North America's leading developers of quality resources that encourage, assist, and equip parents to build Christian faith in their families. Lightwave's products help parents answer their children's questions about the Christian faith, teach them how to make church, Sunday school, and Bible reading more meaningful for their children, provide them with pointers on teaching their children to pray, and much, much more.

Lightwave, together with its various publishing and ministry partners, such as Focus on the Family, has been successfully producing innovative books, music, and games since 1984. Some of its more recent products include the *Parents' Guide to the Spiritual Growth of Children*, *My Time With God*, and *Mealtime Moments*.

Lightwave also has a fun kids' Web site and an Internet-based newsletter called *Tips and Tools for Spiritual Parenting*. For more information and a complete list of Lightwave products, please visit: **www.lightwavepublishing.com**.